Foreign Language Teaching

THE LIBRARY OF EDUCATION

A Project of The Center for Applied Research in Education, Inc.

G. R. Gottschalk, Director

Categories of Coverage

I	II	III
Curriculum and Teaching	Administration, Organization, and Finance	Psychology for Educators

IV	V	VI
History, Philosophy, and Social Foundations	Professional Skills	Educational Institutions

Foreign Language Teaching

J. WESLEY CHILDERS

Chairman, Department of Modern Languages
Parsons College

The Center for Applied Research in Education, Inc.
New York

LIBRARY OF CONGRESS
CATALOG CARD NO.: 64-16035

PRINTED IN THE UNITED STATES OF AMERICA

Foreword

Now, more than at any previous time in our history, there is a sense of urgency in the teaching of modern foreign languages. This urgency is felt because American education has taken on international dimensions and is being redesigned in terms of the needs of a free nation in an interdependent world. Learning to understand, speak, and read one or more modern foreign languages is an integral part of education for citizenship competency.

To make modern foreign languages an integral and meaningful part of general education will require a sense of urgency and assiduous effort as well. Professor Childers' account of the status and growth of foreign language teaching in the United States will help illuminate the task ahead by giving a factual basis for assessing the present situation and by reviewing some of the ideological roots of the current progress in language development. It will give to all concerned with the renaissance of language teaching and learning an awareness of circumstances prevailing in the early 1960's—circumstances, such as the following, which present a direct challenge to the educational statesmen of tomorrow:

1. Students in many schools have no opportunity to study a modern foreign language because none is offered.

2. Modern foreign language offerings are for the most part restricted to Spanish, French, or other West European languages, and these languages are being studied by an insufficient number of students.

3. Language courses are generally too short for substantial accomplishment. Most communities lack a continuum of language instruction that begins in the elementary or junior high school and extends in uninterrupted sequence through the senior high school.

4. Language requirements and standards of achievement do not correspond to the realities of the national need for large numbers of people in all professions and occupations to have foreign language competence in addition to their primary field of specialization.

5. Too few qualified teachers are presently available or being prepared to provide instruction consistent with today's language objectives.

6. The organization and administration of foreign language instruction is not keeping pace with advances in our knowledge of language and language-learning processes.

These and other considerations are in fact motivating much support and improvement of the teaching of modern foreign languages at all levels, from elementary school through graduate school and in adult education.

MARJORIE C. JOHNSTON
Director, Instructional Resources Branch
U.S. Office of Education

Foreign Language Teaching

J. Wesley Childers

The purpose of this important volume in the Library of Education is threefold: (1) to give a brief history of the changing status of foreign language teaching in the schools and colleges of the United States, (2) to highlight the principal methods of teaching foreign language today, (3) to review research which has been done in the foreign language field and to show how this research has influenced the teaching of languages.

Although there is some consideration of language teaching prior to the twentieth century, the chief time span in the book is from 1900 to 1963.

This book on the curriculum and teaching of foreign languages is one of several that cover the field of language in the Library series. It is a fascinating story of the "ups and downs" of foreign language teaching in American schools, and it documents the substantial and prominent place that the teaching of foreign language now holds in the curriculum. The author has effectively and authoritatively presented the need for language teaching and the tested practices for both elementary and secondary schools.

WALTER A. ANDERSON
Content Editor

Contents

CHAPTER I

Rise and Fall of the Classical Languages

Position of the Classics in Colonial Schools

Foreign language teaching in the United States began in colonies along the eastern seaboard shortly after their founding. The English settlers brought with them their educational traditions, which centered in private schools and colleges, and transplanted them to the New World. Since most of the earliest private schools in the colonies were established to educate young gentlemen for careers in theology, medicine, law, and letters, their "classical" education consisted of Latin, Greek, geometry, history, natural philosophy, and science.

The French and German settlers established their own private schools and began to have French and German taught to their children. These modern languages, however, did not supplant Latin and Greek as languages for college entrance or for graduation from college. In fact, until the nineteenth century few colleges gave students credit for studying modern foreign languages.

From the time of the Renaissance, classical languages had been considered the great medium for carrying on the humanistic tradition in Europe. Latin, especially, was the universal language of oral or written communication among scholars. It was the language of the church, of the state, of law, and of other professions. Young men were taught the classical languages in private schools in order to prepare them for professional studies in colleges. Emphasis was on the content and style of the Latin masterpieces so that aspiring ministers, lawyers, teachers, or writers would acquire a correctness of form and an elegance of expression. This humanistic concept of Latin continued in the twentieth century.

Position of the Classics in the Twentieth Century

At the beginning of the twentieth century, American secondary schools and colleges generally based their curricular offerings on

1

those of the English, French, and German schools. In the language fields Latin and Greek were offered, but very little work was offered in the modern foreign languages. American society was largely rural until after World War I, and many students who began secondary school studies had to drop out to work on farms. Those who were able to complete a secondary curriculum in public or private schools usually studied Latin or Greek, if they studied any foreign language. Since some of the principal colleges and universities required Latin or Greek as an entrance or graduation requirement, and since modern foreign languages were held in low esteem, the college-bound high school students usually studied classical languages. Furthermore, these classical languages were said to give the students a mental discipline not found in the modern languages. In 1900, Latin enrolled 50.6 per cent of the total public high school population in grades 9–12.

The Modern Language Association of America, founded in 1883 by United States language teachers and scholars, had little effect, if any, on the pattern of language offerings in the American schools during the first decade of the twentieth century. By insisting on making modern language study respectable, difficult, and disciplinary, with emphasis on grammatical analysis and a philological approach, the MLA was following, not changing, the current practices in language teaching at that time. Latin continued to be the chief language studied in high schools and colleges, with German a growing but far-distant second, and French a weak third. As late as 1910, almost half (49 per cent) of the high school pupils in grades 9–12 were enrolled in Latin classes, 23.7 per cent in German classes, and 9.9 per cent in French classes. By 1915, the per cent of high school students enrolled in Latin had declined to 37.3, a figure which was still higher than the 35.9 per cent for all of the modern foreign languages combined. The 1915 per cents for modern foreign languages were: German, 24.4; French, 8.8; and Spanish, 2.7.

The per cents for students studying Latin (in the total high school population) declined after World War I, despite the efforts of the American Classical League (founded in 1918) to encourage the study of the classics. By 1922, Latin and the modern foreign language enrollments were about equal in per cents of the total high school population: 27.5 to 27.4, respectively. Of the total 27.4 per cent in modern languages, French accounted for 15.5 per cent; Spanish, 11.3 per cent; and German, only six-tenths of one per cent.[1] (Chapter II will trace the effect of World War I on modern foreign languages.) After 1934, Latin enrollments declined until they reached a low of 6.9 per cent of the high school population in 1954. Latin, however, continued to surpass any single modern foreign language offered in the public secondary schools until after World War II, when Spanish overtook it.

According to a 1959 Modern Language Association survey, Latin continued to be the leading foreign language in independent or private secondary schools of the United States.[2] The per cents for languages enrolling over one per cent of the total independent-school population were: Latin, 38.4; French, 24.8; Spanish, 13.0; German, 3.5; and Greek, 1.1.

Ancient Greek had almost disappeared from the public high schools by 1960. A total of 222 pupils of Greek were reported in that year from five states: Indiana, Kansas, Louisiana, Massachusetts, and Rhode Island.

The fluctuations in public secondary school enrollments in Latin and in modern foreign languages from 1890 through 1960 are shown in Table 1. Although the per cent of high school students studying Latin declined sharply after 1910, more students were studying Latin in 1934 (899,300) when the per cent was 16.0 than in 1910 (448,383) when the per cent was 49.0. Likewise, more students were enrolled in Latin in 1960 (661,563) when the per cent was 7.6 than in 1900 (262,752) when the per cent was 50.6. The explanation is that the population of public high schools (9–12) increased from about one-half million (519,251) in 1900 to 8,649,495 in 1960—an enormous gain of 8,130,244, or a 1,566 per cent of increase. It is obvious that in 1960 no one foreign language could enroll such a large per cent of the total high school population as Latin did in 1900, when the number of high school students was small, and when Latin was the chief language for

---

[1] The per cents for Latin and the modern foreign languages, 1900–1948, are derived from William R. Parker, *The National Interest and Foreign Languages,* U.S. National Commission for the United Nations Educational, Scientific, and Cultural Organization, 3rd ed. (Washington, D.C.: U.S. Government Printing Office, 1961), pp. 85–86.

[2] John Harmon, "Foreign Languages in Independent Secondary Schools, Fall 1959," in *Reports of Surveys and Studies in the Teaching of Modern Foreign Languages* (New York: Modern Language Association, 1961), p. 35.

college-oriented students. The 1960 enrollments in Latin were 7.6 per cent of the total high school population, ranking Latin in third position, surpassed only by Spanish (10.8 per cent) and French (8.6 per cent).

TABLE 1

ENROLLMENTS IN LATIN, WITH PER CENTS OF TOTAL HIGH SCHOOL
POPULATION (9–12) AND OF TOTAL FOREIGN LANGUAGE
ENROLLMENTS

Year	Total High School Population (9–12)	Latin Enrollment[a]	Per Cent Latin in High School Population	Total Foreign Language Enrollments[b]	Per Cent Latin in Foreign Language enrollments
1890	202,963	70,429	34.7	103,518	68.0
1895	350,099	153,693	43.9	216,378	71.0
1900	519,251	262,752	50.6	377,517	69.6
1905	679,702	341,215	50.2	540,368	63.1
1910	915,061	448,383	49.0	762,273	58.8
1915	1,328,984	495,711	37.3	972,821	51.0
1922	2,230,000	613,250	27.5	1,224,275	50.1
1928	3,354,473	737,984	22.0	1,583,322	46.6
1934	5,620,626	899,300	16.0	1,995,322	45.1
1948	5,399,452	421,174	7.8	1,161,974	36.2
1954[c]	6,582,300	454,179	6.9	1,388,866	32.7
1958	7,897,232	617,500	7.8	1,916,187	32.2
1959	8,155,573	639,776	7.8	2,204,884	29.0
1960	8,649,495	661,563	7.6	2,534,509	26.1

[a] Latin and total FL enrollments from 1890 through 1948 are estimated from per cents of the total high school population given by William R. Parker, *The National Interest and Foreign Languages*, 1961, pp. 85–86. (See footnote 1.)

[b] Latin plus modern foreign languages.

[c] Latin and FL enrollments have been estimated for 48 states, based on the following data gathered by Donald D. Walsh from 41 states: Latin, 310,891; per cent Latin in HSP, 6.9; FL enrollments, 950,664; per cent FL enrollments in HSP, 21.1.

CHAPTER II

Effects of Wars and Politics
on Modern Foreign Languages

Before the Revolutionary War, French, German, and Spanish were established as the "traditional" modern foreign languages in the North American educational system. Early French settlers in Canada founded church-related schools in which missionary priests taught children the language and culture of France, together with other school subjects. A few of these missionaries came down into the New England colonies to teach French in private schools. Well-to-do English settlers in the South and in New England also brought governesses or tutors with them to instruct their children in French or German. German settlers, invited by William Penn, came into Pennsylvania in the last two decades of the seventeenth century, establishing their own denominational schools in which the German language was taught. Jesuit missionaries in the present states of Florida, Texas, New Mexico, and California taught Spanish to children in mission schools, as well as in private homes. A brief history of the teaching of each of these three languages is given later in this chapter.

After the Revolutionary War French was the most popular modern foreign language in private schools and colleges in the colonies along the Atlantic coast, with the exception of Florida. Because France gave military aid to the colonists in their revolt against England, a wave of good will toward France and its culture was reflected in the increased study of French after the Revolutionary War.

In the nineteenth century when, through purchases and conquests, the United States extended its borders from the Atlantic to the Pacific, and when millions of new immigrants swarmed to America, French continued to be the chief modern foreign language in the East; German, in Pennsylvania and in the Midwest; and Spanish, in Florida, the Southwest, and the West.

5

From 1900 to 1917, modern foreign language study in the United States on secondary and college levels was largely restricted to German and French, with some scattered offerings in Italian and Spanish. At the time of World War II, Chinese, Japanese, Portuguese, and Russian were added in special programs at the college level. After 1957, Russian became more of an established language, both in secondary schools and in colleges, and certain other languages were declared "critical" to the national defense.

Interest and enrollments in any particular foreign language rose or fell, like mercury in a thermometer, in proportion to America's warmth of approval or chill of disapproval in regard to the prestige, power, or political influence of the nation whose language was being studied. German was the first modern foreign language to feel this mercurial quality of the American political and social climate. However, French and Spanish, the other principal modern foreign languages taught in American schools and colleges, have also had their ups and downs.

German

German in early American schools.[1]   German was taught in Colonial America toward the end of the seventeenth century. In 1683 William Penn invited certain religious sects to come to Pennsylvania in order to find religious freedom; and groups of Dunkers, Lutherans, Mennonites, and Moravians responded to his invitation. The early German settlers established denominational, Latin-grammar schools in which German was also taught. Germantown, Pennsylvania, was a main center, but many Germans moved into Georgia, the Carolinas, and New York. German became the principal modern foreign language in the Middle Colonies. In 1749 the Academy at Philadelphia, established by Benjamin Franklin, offered German.

Other waves of German immigrants came to the United States in 1830 and 1848 as a result of revolutions in Germany and in other parts of Europe. The schools which these immigrants established were largely nondenominational, designed to transplant the German

---

[1] Information on modern foreign language teaching in early American schools comes largely from E. W. Bagster-Collins, "History of Modern Language Teaching in the United States," in *Studies in Modern Language Teaching* (New York: The Macmillan Company, 1930), pp. 6–31, 49–57.

type of education to America. The success of the Prussian school system after 1830 stimulated the founding of a German type of education in the New World. These German schools were expanded rapidly when more than 500,000 immigrants arrived between 1852–54, and when more than an annual increase of 150,000 occurred between 1866–73. In all, over 6,000,000 German immigrants came to the United States between 1820 and 1910.[2]

Many large cities established the teaching of German in the public elementary schools around 1850. Cincinnati was one of the earliest to offer parallel classes by teachers of English and German. Other cities tried this form of bilingualism but had to abandon it because it proved to be too expensive. Chief cities in which German was taught in the elementary schools were Baltimore, Buffalo, Chicago, Cleveland, Dayton, Denver, Indianapolis, Milwaukee, New York City, Saint Louis, San Francisco, and Toledo. By 1870 New York City offered German in all eight grades, with an enrollment in German of approximately 20,000 pupils.

In secondary schools of the nineteenth century German was offered in some of the Eastern academies as an optional subject, but the enrollments were never large. Latin and Greek were still the chief foreign languages studied. New York State had 156 academies in 1848, with German taught in only 18. A few public high schools in the East began to offer German around 1850. By contrast, in the Midwest 50 per cent of the public high schools offered German between 1860–1900.

German made its appearance in the curriculum of colleges in 1779 at William and Mary College. Harvard had a licensed German teacher, Meno Poehls, in 1816, and another, Charles Follen, in 1825. George Blaetterman taught German at the University of Virginia from 1825 to 1840. Other colleges which introduced German in the first half of the nineteenth century were Amherst (1824), Bowdoin (1826), Columbia (1830), and Yale (1831). By the middle of the nineteenth century many colleges and universities established the Bachelor of Science degree as a parallel with the Bachelor of Arts, permitting students who elected German instead

---

[2] Edwin H. Zeydel, "The Teaching of German in the United States from Colonial Times to the Present," *Reports of Surveys and Studies in the Teaching of Modern Foreign Languages* (New York: Modern Language Association, 1961), p. 293.

of Latin or Greek to take the Bachelor of Science degree. The University of Michigan, for example, established the B.S. degree in 1853. Johns Hopkins set up the scientific or philological study of German in 1875. German and other modern languages, however, were of slight importance in institutions of higher learning until after the 1870's, when the elective system in many colleges gave them a chance to compete on favorable terms with Latin and Greek.

German in the twentieth century. At the beginning of the twentieth century, German universities and German culture enjoyed high prestige. American scholars studied in German universities, and German professors came to America to set up programs of graduate studies patterned after those of Germany. The German immigrants in the United States—who had usually settled in the East, in northern sections of the Midwest, and in the Far West—were respected citizens of their communities. They had succeeded in establishing German as the principal foreign language in public secondary schools and in private academies. Enrollments in German were 14.3 per cent of the total public high school population in 1900, and 24.4 per cent in 1915.[3] Many communities also were teaching German in the elementary grades. German seemed to have a secure and favored place in the American educational system. But this was before April 6, 1917; after that date, there was a different story to tell.

World War I. The entry of the United States into the war against Germany and the Central Powers in 1917 touched off a wave of hysteria over the entire country. Stories of German atrocities were printed in most of the newspapers and were repeated from pulpits and platforms; the German language was dropped from high schools and colleges; and the teaching of German was declared illegal by the legislatures of 22 separate states. German enrollments plummeted from a high of 24.4 per cent of the public high school population in 1915 to a low of .6 per cent by 1922. This distrust of Germany was stated vividly by William Parker:[4]

> Almost overnight Americans developed a hysterical distrust of all things German—hence, by emotional logic, of most things "foreign."

---

[3] E. W. Bagster-Collins, "History of Modern Language Teaching in the United States," in *Studies in Modern Language Teaching* (New York: The Macmillan Company, 1930), p. 32.

[4] William Parker, *The National Interest and Foreign Languages*, p. 85.

Twenty-two states even went so far as to pass laws hostile to foreign language instruction. These were eventually reversed by the Supreme Court (1923), but the mood that produced them remained, and in the 1920's and 1930's our isolationist temper was rationalized and made to seem educationally respectable by new theories of what the child in a democracy should be taught.

The fact that all modern foreign languages suffered when German was banished from American schools is documented by Parker [5] and discussed by Zeydel.[6] Zeydel states that the language needs of World War II and the added needs imposed by our competition with Russia have not, up to the present, "fully restored the study of languages to their rightful place in the curriculum, especially in the secondary schools." He underscores his belief by stating:

> It is to be hoped that the language teachers will take this lesson to heart and never lose sight of the fact that they are first and foremost teachers of the modern foreign languages, and not of French, German, Italian, Russian, Spanish, or any other single language or group of them.[7]

Reestablishing German as a primary modern foreign language has been difficult. Secondary school enrollments in German rose from .6 per cent of the public high school population in 1922 to 1.8 per cent in 1928; by 1934 the per cent was 2.4. When the U.S. Office of Education made its survey of the secondary schools in 1948, German was down again below one per cent (.8). This second fall in enrollments reflected America's entry into World War II against Germany and her allies.

German in colleges. The colleges maintained a calmer attitude toward the teaching of German during World War II than did the secondary schools, but since many students of college age were away at war, college enrollments in German dropped between 1941 and 1945. When the veterans who had been in Europe returned to their campuses in the United States, they brought a renewed interest in the study of German. The Appleton-Century-

---

[5] Parker, *op. cit.*, p. 86.

[6] Edwin H. Zeydel, "The Teaching of German in the United States from Colonial Times to the Present," in *Reports of Surveys and Studies in the Teaching of Modern Foreign Languages* (New York: Modern Language Association, 1961), p. 297.

[7] *Ibid.*, p. 299.

TABLE 2

ENROLLMENTS IN GERMAN, WITH PER CENTS OF
TOTAL PUBLIC HIGH SCHOOL POPULATION (9–12)
AND OF TOTAL MODERN FOREIGN LANGUAGES

Year	Total High School Population (9–12)	German[a] Enrollment	Per Cent German in High School Population	Enrollment in Modern Foreign Languages[a]	Per Cent German in Modern Foreign Languages
1890	202,963	21,311	10.5	33,089	64.4
1895	350,099	39,911	11.4	62,685	63.7
1900	519,251	74,252	14.3	114,765	64.7
1905	679,702	137,299	20.2	199,153	68.9
1910	915,061	216,869	23.7	313,890	69.1
1915	1,328,984	324,272	24.4	477,110	68.0
1922	2,230,000	13,385	0.6	611,025	2.2
1928	3,354,473	60,381	1.8	845,338	7.1
1934	5,620,626	134,897	2.4	1,096,022	12.3
1948	5,399,452	43,195	0.8	740,800	5.8
1954[b]	6,582,300	52,656	0.8	934,687	5.6
1958	7,897,232	93,054	1.2	1,298,687	7.2
1959	8,155,573	123,581	1.5	1,564,883	7.9
1960	8,649,495	151,261	1.7	1,872,946	8.1

[a] The German and total MFL enrollments from 1890 through 1948 are estimated from per cents of the languages in the total high school population given by William R. Parker, *The National Interest and Foreign Languages*, pp. 85–86.
[b] The German and MFL enrollments have been estimated for 48 States, based on the following data gathered by Donald D. Walsh from 41 States: German, 36,-043; per cent German in HSP, 0.8; MFL, 639,773; per cent MFL in HSP, 14.2.

Crofts reports [8] on German enrollments in colleges and universities (1946–1959) showed an increase of 108 per cent in 1946, another increase of 11.26 per cent in 1947, decreases from 1948 through 1952, and increases every year from 1953 through 1959. The Appleton-Century-Crofts report from 657 institutions in 1959 showed that German enrollments had increased 13.6 per cent over those of 1958. The Modern Language Association survey of 1,039 institutions for 1958 and 1959 showed a 12.9 per cent of increase.[9] Similar MLA surveys for 1960 and 1961 showed the following per cents of increase in German four-year college enrollments: 1959 to 1960,

[8] Appleton-Century-Crofts, "Modern Language News," 1946–59.
[9] Mara Vamos, *et al.*, "Modern Foreign Language Enrollments in Four-Year Accredited Colleges and Universities, Fall 1958 and Fall 1959," in *Reports of Surveys and Studies in the Teaching of Modern Foreign Languages* (New York: Modern Language Association, 1961), p. 55.

9.1; 1960 to 1961, 11.7. In 1960, German enrollments were 24.4 per cent of the total modern foreign language enrollments in these institutions; in 1961 they were 24.1 per cent—behind French (38.0%) and Spanish (28.5%).[10]

On the junior college level, Modern Language Association surveys of 1959–61 revealed the following per cents of increase in German enrollments from approximately 600 accredited two-year colleges: 1959 to 1960, 10.5; 1960 to 1961, 17.8. German enrollments in junior colleges were 19.6 per cent of all modern foreign language enrollments in those institutions in 1960, and had increased to 19.9 per cent in 1961.[11]

French

Early American schools.[12]   French was taught in private schools almost from the beginning of colonial America. Early French explorers had established trading posts and forts in Canada, along the Great Lakes, and down the Mississippi and Ohio river valleys from Detroit to New Orleans.

After Louis XIV of France revoked the Edict of Nantes in 1685, many French Huguenots fled from France to England, The Netherlands, Germany, Switzerland, and America. In America they settled in North and South Carolina, with Charleston as their center; in Pennsylvania, around Philadelphia; in New York State, around New York City and at New Paltz. The earliest recorded, licenced teacher of French in New York City was Andrew Faucautt, September 13, 1703. Prudent de la Fayole was licensed on August 29, 1705. It is thought that these two men started a school chiefly for children of the French émigrés.

Interest in France and French culture was high among the educated American colonists in the eighteenth century because of the

---

10 John Harmon and Hannelore Tierney, *Modern Foreign Language Enrollments in Four-Year Colleges and Universities, Fall 1961* (New York: Modern Language Association, 1962), p. 3.

11 J. Wesley Childers and Barbara Bates Bell, *Modern Foreign Language Teaching in Junior Colleges, Fall, 1961* (New York: Modern Language Association, 1962), pp. 6–7.

12 Information on the teaching of French in the early American schools comes largely from E. W. Bagster-Collins, "History of Modern Language Teaching in the United States," in *Studies in Modern Language Teaching* (New York: The Macmillan Company, 1930), pp. 3–96.

exciting ideas of the French philosophers, especially those of Montesquieu, whose *Spirit of Laws* was sold in English translation at Charleston, South Carolina, in 1750, two years after its publication in France. Also, leaders of the movement for independence from England were Francophiles. After France actively supported the American colonists by sending troops and supplies during the Revolutionary War, interest in the study of French increased in American schools.

Early American teaching of French was in private schools or in private homes. Often the teachers went to the homes of students, especially if they were adults, and classes were often held in the evenings. In many communities these classes became social events. The major part of the teaching, however, was done in private day schools. After 1750, many French boarding schools were established in major Eastern cities.

The development of private academies was a phenomenon of the middle and late eighteenth century. Benjamin Franklin founded the Philadelphia Academy in 1749; in 1754 a Mr. Creamer was engaged to teach French and German there. The Rev. J. Peter Tetard had a French boarding school in New York City in 1774. In 1778 Phillips Andover Academy was founded, and in 1781, Phillips Exeter Academy. There were 150 academies in New England by 1830.

Academies in New York State were in existence in 1784 and were given legal status in 1787. Four of these taught French in 1787, according to the Regents' report for that year. By 1807, there were 22 academies in New York State; four offered French, with a total enrollment of 38 pupils. By 1845, French was taught in 124 of the 153 New York academies. There were over 200 academies in North Carolina between 1800 and 1840; several of them offered French. Illinois had three academies in 1818, and by 1848 there were approximately 125; French was offered in only a few of them.

The popularity and prestige of French suffered reverses in America between 1830 and 1870. The classicists assailed French as an inferior language, checking its growth in many schools. Local opposition to French arose because of the writings of the "atheistic" Voltaire. French political unrest in the first part of the nineteenth century and France's attempt to dominate Mexico during the Civil

War in the United States caused the American ardor for France to cool somewhat. As has been discussed already, the interest in German culture took an upswing during this period, especially after Germany defeated France in 1870–71.

French in public high schools. Public high schools were established in the nineteenth century, the earliest being the English Classical High School of Boston in 1821. French was an elective or optional course for girls in the last two years of the high school curriculum at the Boston High School for Girls in 1826, as well as in the English Classical High School there. In 1847 Hartford, Connecticut, had 95 high school students of French. Many more high schools in Connecticut were offering French between 1851–62, but the total French enrollment for the state in 1862 was 132 pupils. Between 1857 and 1898 French was required by law to be offered in Massachusetts towns of over 4,000. It could substitute for Greek, especially in the girls' schools. Although French was the popular modern foreign language in Eastern high schools, enrollments were low. Tuition was charged at first in the Eastern high schools, and French instruction was offered "at the expense of the pupil." In the period 1849–51 at the Lowell, Massachusetts, High School, 59 per cent of the girls took French; three per cent of the boys elected it. Baltimore Central High School introduced French in 1852; Dubuque, Iowa, in 1858. Few schools in the Midwest, however, taught French before the twentieth century.

French in the elementary schools never became an integral part of the public school system. It was introduced into the elementary schools of a few large city systems after 1850: New York City, 1854; San Francisco, 1867; Boston, 1895; and a few other New England cities by 1901. The current French programs in elementary schools, however, are largely a phenomenon of the 1950's and later (see Chapter IV).

French teaching in American colleges and universities started in the eighteenth century, but it was not given definite status until about the time of the Civil War. Harvard had a teacher of French, Louis Langloisserie, in 1735, and another, Joyan Jensen Berg, in 1766. In 1826 George Ticknor was permitted to teach some "volunteers" who took French without credit. With the change to the elective system of studies at Harvard in 1870, French received a definite place in the curriculum. Amherst and Yale had put French on a definite basis in 1864.

Other institutions of higher learning which were offering French before 1830 were William and Mary (1779), Columbia (1784), Williams College (1792), University of North Carolina (1795), Union College (1802), Princeton (1806), Bowdoin (1820), Amherst (1824), University of Virginia (1825), and Yale (1825). With the establishment of the B.S. degree after 1850, in many major colleges and universities French began to share with German the language requirement for this degree.

The influence of wars on enrollments in the twentieth century. The fluctuations of enrollments in French during the twentieth century reflected the fortunes of wars, as well as political and social considerations. After Germany defeated France in 1870–71, French prestige and influence sank to a low point in America. The secondary school enrollments in French and German at the end of the nineteenth century and until 1917 show the relative prestige of the French and German cultures in America at that time. In 1890, French enrollments constituted 5.8 per cent of the high school population; in 1900, 7.8; and in 1915, 8.8. German enrollment per cents for the same three years were 10.5, 14.3, and 24.4.

After April, 1917, enrollments in French soared when the teaching of German practically disappeared from the American schools. The 1922 survey of enrollments showed French with 15.5 per cent of the high school population, and German with only .6 per cent.

FRENCH AND GERMAN ENROLLMENT PER CENTS OF HIGH SCHOOL
POPULATION (9–12) [13]

Year	French	German
1890	5.8	10.5
1900	7.8	14.3
1915	8.8	24.4
1922	15.5	.6

French remained in first place as the principal secondary school foreign language until approximately 1940, when the tide of war again caused a lowering of French prestige in the United States. When France fell in 1940 to the short German *blitzkrieg,* an emo-

---

[13] From William Parker, *National Interest and Foreign Languages,* pp. 85–86, based on Bagster-Collins, *History of Modern Language Teaching in the United States,* pp. 32–34.

tional wave of resentment toward France swept over the American people. In protest against French capitulation, many high school students dropped the study of French and enrolled in Spanish. Teachers of French suddenly found themselves assigned to teach Spanish classes. Spanish replaced French as the chief secondary school foreign language, and it has maintained this rank up to the present time. By 1954, however, the gap between French and Spanish enrollments in public high schools began to narrow. French enrollments had received added stimulus from two important sources: (1) secondary school guidance counselors who advised college-bound students to study French rather than Spanish, and (2) the vigorous and successful teaching of French in the elementary schools, which assumed national proportions when the medium of television was widely used in the 1960's.

TABLE 3

ENROLLMENTS IN FRENCH, WITH PER CENTS OF TOTAL HIGH SCHOOL
POPULATION (9–12) AND OF TOTAL MODERN FOREIGN LANGUAGES

Year	Total High School Population (9–12)	French[a] Enrollment	Per Cent French in High School Population	Enrollment in Modern Foreign Languages[a]	Per Cent French in Modern Foreign Languages
1890	202,963	11,772	5.8	33,089	35.6
1895	350,099	22,757	6.5	62,685	36.3
1900	519,251	40,503	7.8	114,765	35.3
1905	679,702	61,852	9.1	199,153	31.1
1910	915,061	90,591	9.9	313,890	28.9
1915	1,328,984	116,957	8.8	477,110	24.5
1922	2,230,000	345,650	15.5	611,025	56.6
1928	3,354,473	469,626	14.0	845,338	55.6
1934	5,620,626	612,648	10.9	1,096,022	55.9
1948	5,399,452	253,781	4.7	740,800	34.3
1954[b]	6,582,300	368,609	5.6	934,687	39.4
1958	7,897,232	479,769	6.1	1,298,687	36.9
1959	8,155,573	603,733	7.4	1,564,883	38.6
1960	8,649,495	747,486	8.6	1,872,946	39.9

[a] The French and total MFL enrollments from 1890 through 1948 are estimated from per cents of the languages in the total high school population given by William R. Parker, *The National Interest and Foreign Languages*, 1962, pp. 85–86.

[b] The French and MFL enrollments have been estimated for 48 States, based on the following data gathered by Donald D. Walsh from 41 States: French, 252,306; per cent French in HSP, 5.6; MFL, 639,773; per cent MFL in HSP, 14.2.

French teaching in colleges and universities took an upswing after 1917, when German offerings were curtailed or dropped. In the 1920's and 1930's the French language, literature, and way of life had a great appeal for American intellectuals. Many students enrolled in French courses in the United States; others went to France to study. Artists and writers took up residence in France whenever possible. There were many exchanges of American and French professors and students. Yet during these same years, because of the growing emphasis on vocational courses in the high schools and an indifference on the part of many school boards toward offering foreign languages in the public schools, many colleges found it necessary to drop the foreign language entrance requirement, and many others dropped the language requirement for the B.A. degree.

Lower French enrollments in colleges reflected the public apathy toward languages. France's defeat by Germany in 1940, and the emotional reaction against the French, caused college students to abandon the study of the French language, just as it had caused high school students to do. The Appleton-Century-Crofts reports on college enrollments in modern foreign languages show a per cent of decrease in fall French enrollments (1941–43) for each succeeding year: 1941, 23.5; 1942, 23.7; 1943, 21.4. There were per cents of increase from 1944 through 1947, reaching a high of 68.4 in the fall of 1946 when thousands of World War II veterans enrolled in American colleges and universities. French enrollments declined again from 1948 through 1951, but they have shown per cents of increase every year since 1952.[14]

French occupied first place in modern foreign language enrollments in four-year colleges in 1961,[15] having shown sizable per cents of increase for three consecutive years: 1958 to 1959, 14; 1959 to 1960, 13.7; and 1960 to 1961, 14.4. French had 38 per cent of the total modern foreign language enrollments in these institutions in 1961.

In junior colleges, French had 36.5 per cent of modern foreign language enrollments in 1961, placing it second to Spanish (38.1 per cent). The per cents of increase in French enrollments, however,

14 Appleton-Century-Crofts, "Modern Language News," 1941–1959.
15 From John Harmon and Hannelore Tierney, *Modern Foreign Language Enrollments in Four-Year Colleges and Universities, Fall 1961*, pp. 1–3.

had been consistently better than those for Spanish for two consecutive years: 1959 to 1960, 18.9; 1960 to 1961, 15.3. Spanish per
cents of increase for these two years were 14.1 and 13.8.[16] It appears
likely that before 1970 French enrollments in the junior colleges
will overtake those of Spanish.

Spanish

Wars create interest in Spanish.   Before 1900, the teaching of
Spanish in the high schools of the United States was largely confined to the South, Southwest, and West, where the proximity to
Cuba and Mexico stimulated an interest in learning to speak Spanish. On the college level, instruction in Spanish had a long and, at
times, a brilliant history during the nineteenth century in a few
colleges scattered along the Atlantic coast, the principal ones being
Bowdoin, Harvard, Pennsylvania, University (College) of the City
of New York, and the University of Virginia.[17]
   Two wars in the nineteenth century created an interest in Hispanic culture and boosted offerings in Spanish, both in secondary
schools and in colleges: the war with Mexico (1848) and the Span-
ish-American War (1898). After the Mexican War, the University
of Michigan, the Naval Academy at Annapolis, and the United
States Military Academy at West Point began serious programs in
Spanish. After the war with Spain, Spanish language and literature
courses proliferated in high schools and colleges. By 1910, Spanish
enrollments in secondary schools were measurable, constituting .7
per cent of the total public high school students; by 1915, the per
cent had increased to 2.7.
   Peaceful stimuli to interest in Spanish.   Four events in the early
part of the twentieth century were destined to change slowly the
attitude toward Spanish and Hispanic culture: (1) the founding of
the Hispanic Society of America by Mr. Archer Huntington in 1904;
(2) the establishing of the American Association of Teachers of
Spanish and Portuguese (1917); (3) the beginning of the Middlebury Spanish School (1917); and (4) the founding of the Instituto

---

16 J. Wesley Childers and Barbara Bates Bell, *Modern Foreign Language Teaching in Junior Colleges, Fall 1961*, p. 7.
17 See Sturgis E. Leavitt, "The Teaching of Spanish in the United States," in
Reports of Surveys and Studies in the Teaching of Modern Foreign Languages
(New York: Modern Language Association), pp. 309–326.

de las Españas (now Casa Hispánica) at Columbia University (1920).[18]

World War I. With the collapse of German enrollments in 1917, and with the withdrawal of England and Germany from trade with Latin America after 1914, enrollments in Spanish boomed. By 1922 the enrollments in secondary schools had climbed to 11.3 per cent of the high school population. High school and college students were advised to study Spanish for two chief reasons which proved to be detrimental to its scholarship and prestige: (1) Spanish is "easy"; (2) Spanish is a "practical" language for business with South America. Much disillusionment resulted when thousands of students discovered that the demands of Spanish were as rigorous as those of other modern languages, and when other thousands realized that they would never be engaged in trade with Spanish America. By 1934, the interest in Spanish had sagged; only 6.2 per cent of the high school students were enrolled in Spanish courses. Another war, however, was to send enrollments up again.

World War II. World War II (1939–45) cut off the importation of many raw materials from Europe and Asia into the United States and limited American exports to those areas. The United States turned its attention again to Spanish America, where it could find such commodities as foodstuffs, rubber, tin, and petroleum. Through the efforts of President Franklin Delano Roosevelt, the United States government set up a Good Neighbor Policy with Latin America in 1940, establishing a more cordial social and political relationship. University professors and government officials were sent to Spanish America on cultural or trade missions. By 1948, high school enrollments were up to 8.2 per cent of the total high school population, surpassing French enrollments (4.7 per cent) for the first time. (The surrender of France to Germany in 1940 also hastened the decline of French enrollments.) After the 1940's, Spanish continued to be the most popular language in the public secondary schools, enrolling 10.8 per cent of the high school population (935,418 pupils) in 1960.

Increased demand for Spanish. With the renewed interest of the United States in Latin American economic, social, and political life, as symbolized by the passage of the Alliance for Progress legis-

---

[18] Sturgis Leavitt, *op. cit.,* p. 323.

TABLE 4

ENROLLMENTS IN SPANISH, WITH PER CENTS OF TOTAL HIGH SCHOOL
POPULATION (9–12) AND OF TOTAL MODERN FOREIGN LANGUAGES

Year	Total High School Population (9–12)	Spanish[a] Enrollment	Per Cent Spanish in High School Population	Enrollment in Modern Foreign Languages[a]	Per Cent Spanish in Modern Foreign Languages
1890	202,963			33,089	
1895	350,099			62,685	
1900	519,251			114,765	
1905	679,702			199,153	
1910	915,061	6,406	0.7	313,890	2.0
1915	1,328,984	35,882	2.7	477,110	7.5
1922	2,230,000	252,000	11.3	611,025	41.2
1928	3,354,473	315,329	9.4	845,338	37.3
1934	5,620,626	348,479	6.2	1,096,022	31.8
1948	5,399,452	442,755	8.2	740,800	59.8
1954[b]	6,582,300	480,507	7.3	934,687	51.4
1958	7,897,232	691,024	8.8	1,298,687	53.2
1959	8,155,573	802,266	9.8	1,564,883	51.3
1960	8,649,495	935,418	10.8	1,872,946	49.9

[a] The Spanish and total MFL enrollments from 1890 through 1948 are estimated from per cents of the languages in the total high school population given by William R. Parker, *The National Interest and Foreign Languages*, 1961, pp. 85–86.

[b] The Spanish and MFL enrollments have been estimated for 48 States, based on the following data gathered by Donald D. Walsh from 41 States: Spanish, 330,599; per cent Spanish in HSP, 7.3; MFL enrollments, 639,773; per cent MFL enrollments in HSP, 14.2.

lation in 1960 and the Peace Corps bill in 1961, a knowledge of Spanish appeared to offer thousands of students the opportunities for business or service in Spanish America—opportunities which did not materialize for many students immediately after World War I. In an article titled "Spanish for Business? Yes, Indeed!," [19] Dr. Theodore Huebener pointed out that "Spanish is the language for American business; its commercial value for Americans is far superior to that of any of the other modern languages." [20] The author cited export-import data for seven Latin American nations, using figures from the International Economic Analysis Division, Department of Commerce. He cited several American firms which employ Americans in Latin America, and he mentioned the numerous

[19] *Hispania*, XLVI, No. 2 (May, 1963), 340–41.
[20] *Ibid.*, p. 340.

advertisements in Sunday editions of *The New York Times* for bilingual secretaries, Spanish-speaking tellers, and construction en-
gineers.

Spanish was in great demand in the larger metropolitan areas of
the United States, especially New York City, because of the heavy
migration of the Puerto Ricans to the mainland after World War
II, and the influx of Cubans after 1959. Spanish was needed especially by storekeepers, doctors, nurses, teachers, and clergymen.
Municipalities needed employees who could serve primarily as interpreters and translators.[21] Since Spanish was one of the five official
languages of the United Nations, there were positions for interpreters and translators there. The Foreign Service and the Voice of
America had positions which required a good command of Spanish,
and the Peace Corps sent many Spanish-speaking college graduates
to Latin American countries.

Spanish enrollment in colleges.   In American colleges and universities, Spanish had an uphill fight for respectability in the twentieth century. Many colleges did not permit students to have a major
concentration in Spanish until after 1940. German and French continued to be the preferred languages in graduate schools for masters
and doctoral candidates who were required to demonstrate a reading knowledge of a modern foreign language.

That Spanish had come of age in American colleges and universities after 1940 was amply documented by statistics furnished annually by Appleton-Century-Crofts [22] through 1959, and by the
Modern Language Association later. The Crofts reports (1941–47)
showed that Spanish enrollments had per cents of increase for five
of the seven years (1942 and 1943 showed decreases), with an increase of 27 per cent in 1941 and a high of 56.8 per cent of increase
in 1946. From 1948 through 1952 Spanish enrollments showed per
cents of decrease; since 1952, the enrollments have shown per cents
of increase each year.

The Modern Language Association's reports of enrollments in

21 See John Fletcher Wellemeyer, "Foreign Language Needs of Municipal Employees in Ten Metropolitan Areas," *Reports of Surveys and Studies in the Teaching of Modern Foreign Languages* (New York: Modern Language Association,
1961), pp. 245–52.
22 Appleton-Century-Crofts, "Modern Language News," 1941–59.

modern foreign languages in four-year colleges (1958–61) showed substantial annual increases in Spanish, as did similar reports for two-year colleges (1959–61).[23]

COLLEGE ENROLLMENTS IN SPANISH WITH PER CENTS OF INCREASE

Year	Four-Year Colleges	Per Cent of Increase	Two-Year Colleges	Per Cent of Increase
1958	125,905	–	–	–
1959	137,487	9.2	17,503	–
1960	158,720	12.2	19,969	14.1
1961	179,754	13.3	22,728	13.8

Italian

Before 1900. During the late nineteenth and early twentieth centuries, thousands of Italian immigrants settled in major American cities, especially in those along the Atlantic and Pacific coasts and in cities of the North Central states. These late settlers, finding French, German, Latin, and Spanish entrenched as the traditional foreign languages in the American schools, did not insist that private and public schools offer Italian to their children, in contrast to the way early German settlers had insisted that special German schools be established for their children. Italian, therefore, never became firmly and widely established in American elementary and secondary schools and in colleges. Enrollments in Italian have always been negligible in comparison with those of French, German, and Spanish.

Two explanations may be offered for the small place given to Italian in the American educational system: (1) Most of the Italians who migrated to America in the late nineteenth century spoke regional dialects from southern Italy. Usually there were not enough highly cultured people in any one community interested in making concerted efforts to establish the language of Tuscany (Dante's language) as their common tongue in the American schools. (2) Italo-Americans were victims of social, economic, and political discrimination in many cities, and they quickly tried to "Americanize" themselves by adopting English as their means of communication.

---

[23] For 1958–60, see *Reports of Surveys and Studies in the Teaching of Modern Foreign Languages,* pp. 43–48 and 49–125. For 1961, see the separate MLA reports prepared by John Harmon and Wesley Childers.

In their homes many parents refused to teach Italian to their children, or the latter felt embarrassed because of their European linguistic heritage and refused to learn the language of their parents.

In the nineteenth century, Italian was offered by a few schools in Massachusetts, Connecticut, Rhode Island, and New York, but enrollments were slight. On the college level, William and Mary included Italian before the nineteenth century (1779), because of Thomas Jefferson's interest in establishing a chair of modern languages in his alma mater. Jefferson's interest in Italian (shown by the name *Monticello* which he gave his home in Virginia) was demonstrated again in 1825 when Italian was added to his newly founded University of Virginia. Harvard also offered Italian in 1825; Columbia, in 1826; and Princeton, in 1830. After the Civil War, many additional colleges and universities permitted students to study Italian, some even allowing full credit (instead of half or partial credit), when juniors or seniors elected it.

Secondary school enrollments after 1900. Enrollments in Italian reflected the changing political moods of the twentieth century, as was the case for enrollments in French, German, and Spanish. On the secondary school level, Italian was offered chiefly in five Eastern States: Connecticut, Massachusetts, New Jersey, New York, and Rhode Island. Enrollments were highest in the 1930's before World War II, but they started declining after Italy's entry into the war as an ally of Germany. The continued decline in the 1950's was documented by the Modern Language Association's surveys of 1958 through 1960.[24] The following figures point up the gradual decline in the high schools:

Year	Enrollment in Italian	Per Cent of Change	Per Cent in High School Population	Per Cent of Modern Foreign Languages
1958	22,133	–	0.3	1.7
1959	21,118	–4.6	0.3	1.3
1960	20,026	–5.2	0.2	1.1

Italian in colleges. In the colleges and universities, interest in Italian art, music, literature, and language kept the enrollments fairly steady, yet not very high. This interest in Italian culture in-

24 See J. Wesley Childers, "Foreign Language Offerings and Enrollments in Public Secondary Schools, Fall 1960," in *PMLA*, LXXVII, No. 4 (September, 1962), Part II, p. 3.

creased in the 1950's as American universities established centers in Bologna, Florence, Rome, and other Italian cities. Statistical surveys of the Modern Language Association for 1958–61 reveal the gradual rise in Italian enrollments in four-year, accredited colleges.[25]

Year	Enrollment in Italian	Per Cent of Change	Per Cent of Modern Foreign Languages
1958	9,566	–	2.2
1959	9,975	+4.3	2.1
1960	10,752	+4.6	2.0
1961	12,044	+12.0	1.9

In junior colleges, Italian enrollments were modest in comparison with those of other modern languages: 1959, 391; 1960, 390; and 1961, 610.

Russian

Effects of a cold war. Russian was not taught in many American high schools until after 1957, the date of Russia's successful launching of her space satellite Sputnik I. The United States Office of Education reported that 16 public high schools offered Russian in 1957; 140, in 1958; and 450, in 1959. After 1957, "crash programs" in Russian were set up in some states, and students were encouraged to enroll. In 1958, 26 states reported a total of 4,055 pupils; in 1959, 32 states reported 7,533 (a per cent of increase of 85.5); and in 1960, 36 states enrolled 9,722 pupils, a per cent of increase of 29.4 since 1959 and 139.8 since 1958.

State and federal governmental agencies undertook to prepare secondary school teachers of Russian in anticipation of an expected rapid increase in enrollments. New York State, for example, inaugurated the Russian Language Program through which selected colleges and universities contracted with the state to offer at least 24 semester hours (enough for provisional certification) to regularly employed elementary and secondary school teachers in private and public schools. The participants' fees, tuition, and textbook

[25] See *Reports of Surveys and Studies in the Teaching of Modern Languages,* p. 92, for 1958 and 1959; for 1960 and 1961, see John Harmon's separate survey, *Modern Foreign Language Enrollments in Colleges and Universities, Fall 1961,* p. 3.

costs usually were paid for by the state. The purpose of the Russian Language Program was to prepare experienced teachers of foreign languages (and other academic subjects) to teach Russian whenever the opportunity presented itself in their schools. The state was trying to create a reserve of Russian teachers for future use.

Under Title VI of the National Defense Education Act, institutes were established by the United States Office of Education to train secondary school teachers of Russian. Approximately 500 such teachers were enrolled in summer institutes from 1959 to 1962, and 103 were enrolled in academic-year institutes. One Russian institute was held in the Soviet Union in the summer of 1962, and one again in 1963. A total of six summer Russian institutes were scheduled for 1963 to give training to 188 secondary school teachers. In addition, 30 elementary and secondary school teachers were to be enrolled in one academic-year institute. Secondary schools, however, did not add Russian to the curriculum as fast as had been anticipated; consequently, many persons trained to teach Russian failed to secure teaching positions.

Three factors contributed to the reluctance of some high schools to add Russian. (1) There was the fact of the cold war with Russia and the constant infiltration of Communist propaganda. Textbooks and reading materials ordered from the Soviet Union carried subtle Soviet indoctrination and had to be selected carefully by U.S. Russian teachers. (2) It was difficult to present Russian culture to students, because the pre-1917 culture of Czarist Russia was vastly different from the culture of the post-1917 Soviet Union; and the Communist way of life was incompatible with the American tradition. (3) In the few high schools in which Russian was offered, superintendents reported that the majority of the high school students who were hoping to be admitted to college elected to take French or Spanish because they thought that they could receive higher marks in those languages than they could in Russian. Nevertheless, high school enrollments in Russian did increase, although the total number of students was still small in 1963.

Junior colleges likewise reported increased enrollments in Russian: 1959, 1,544 students; 1960, 1,623 (a per cent increase of 5.1); 1961, 2,108 (a per cent increase of 29.9 since 1960).

Major universities in the United States had offered Russian for many years, but enrollments were low. After 1957, the enrollments

soared briefly (as MLA data for 1958–61 revealed) but tended to
level off to a steady increase similar to that of German.

Year	Enrollment in Russian	Per Cent of Increase	Per Cent of Modern Foreign Languages
1958	16,290	–	3.9
1959	25,491	56.5	5.2
1960	28,947	10.7	5.2
1961	32,104	10.9	5.1

Because of Russian advances in science, many college science
departments were requiring their students to learn to read Russian.
Other students were studying Russian in language and area centers
located at some of the larger universities (see Chapter V). The
cold war with Russia—the competition on military, economic, social, political, and ideological planes—had added another foreign
language to the American schools.

Other Languages

Cold war and nationalism. The second half of the twentieth
century witnessed two powerful forces which influenced the teaching
of non-Western, as well as Western-European languages, in the
United States: (1) the cold war with Russia, as previously mentioned; and (2) the sudden emergence of independent nations in
Africa and Asia.

In the far-flung economic, political, and ideological conflict with
Russia, the United States found itself at a distinct disadvantage in
the area of foreign languages. Russian businessmen, consuls, diplomats, and technical advisers sent to foreign posts were people who
had been thoroughly trained in the language and culture of the
regions to which they were sent. Often these Russians were fluent
speakers of the local dialects of the regions. In most of his foreign
posts, the Russian could live and work among the local people in an
efficient, inconspicuous manner. On the other hand, the American
counterpart usually could not speak the language of the foreign
country to which he was sent, and often he knew very little about
the cultural heritage of the region. The American abroad had to

depend on hiring an interpreter to do his talking for him, and his effectiveness was literally tied to the reliability and competence of the person he engaged.

Because of an inability to communicate with the local populace, the Americans abroad tended to form housing developments or "colonies" exclusively for Americans. This self-imposed living apart from the local people often caused the latter to think that the Americans were rich, arrogant, and snobbish; and American prestige suffered as a consequence.

The special wartime language schools set up by the Armed Forces during World War II (see Chapter III) served to focus the attention of university centers on many non-Western languages. The Foreign Service Institute, established by the United States Congress in 1946, gave the Department of State the responsibility of training its career diplomats in foreign languages. Much of the actual language training in Washington was done under government contract with Georgetown University's Institute of Language and Linguistics. The State Department in 1956 called attention to the urgency of training Foreign Service personnel in foreign languages and gave its officers five years after appointment to acquire a working knowledge of one foreign language. Promotion of junior officers would be held up until they had satisfied this requirement. A further study by the State Department in 1958 pointed up the inadequacy of language proficiency of two-thirds of its Foreign Service officers. The Modern Language Association's surveys of public secondary schools (1954, 1958–60) and of four-year accredited colleges and universities for 1958 to 1961 revealed the effect of past efforts on the status of the unusual or "critical" language enrollments.

Enrollments in Critically Needed Languages

Enrollments in the uncommon or critically needed languages in 1960 comprised only one-half of one per cent of the total public secondary school enrollment in modern foreign languages. The uncommon languages usually were offered by a few public high schools in those states where certain ethnic-group concentrations in large cities created an interest in them. For example, Hebrew, which enrolled 60–79 per cent of the total public secondary school students reported in specified critical languages,[26] had the bulk of its enroll-

---

[26] 1954 (79 per cent), 1958 (72 per cent), 1959 (70 per cent), 1960 (60 per cent).

ments in New York City, where there is a heavy concentration of Jews. Public school enrollments in Hebrew were reported from six additional states: California, Connecticut, Massachusetts, New Jersey, Ohio, and Pennsylvania. Likewise, a concentration of Poles in cities of Connecticut, Illinois, Massachusetts, and Pennsylvania prompted the offering of Polish in a few schools of those states. Portuguese settlements, chiefly in Massachusetts and Rhode Island, accounted for the offering of Portuguese in some of their public high schools. Scandinavian settlers in cities of Illinois, Minnesota, Montana, New York, and Washington created interest in the study of Norwegian and Swedish.

Near Eastern and Oriental languages have also been offered in a few high schools. Utah started the study of Arabic in public secondary schools with an enrollment of 24 students in 1959 and 68 in 1960. California had a few students enrolled in Chinese, as did Hawaii and Illinois. Hawaii, with reported increases in Chinese and Japanese, gave promise of a significant contribution to the total National welfare by training more of its secondary school students in Asiatic languages.

PUBLIC SECONDARY SCHOOL ENROLLMENTS IN CRITICALLY
NEEDED LANGUAGES

	1954 [a] (12 States)	1958 [b] (13 States)	1959 [b] (18 States)	1960 [b] (15 States)
Arabic	–	–	24	68
Chinese	29	21	21	75
Czech	–	7	23	10
Greek (Modern)	–	34	3	14
Hawaiian	–	96	36	132
Hebrew	4,301	4,255	4,262	4,160
Japanese	–	–	63	609
Norwegian	164	210	308	111
Polish	414	499	552	438
Portuguese	384	559	526	600
Swedish	127	228	229	209
Total	5,419	5,909	6,047	6,426

[a] Data from Donald D. Walsh, "Foreign Language Offerings and Enrollments in Public High Schools," *PMLA*, LXX, No. 4, Part II (September, 1955), 55.

[b] Data from MLA surveys conducted by Wesley Childers.

In 1958 and 1959, approximately ninety unusual languages were offered by institutions of higher learning. Enrollments reported for 60 of these showed 8,013 students in 1958 and 9,156 in 1959—an increase of 14.3 per cent. Enrollments from 70 of these critical languages in 1960 were 12,104; and in 1961 there were 14,598 students—an increase of 20.6 per cent from 1960 to 1961. Only 15 of these 70 languages enrolled more than 100 students in 1961: Arabic (693), Chinese (2,200), Czech (192), Dutch (143), Modern Greek (293), Modern Hebrew (4,250), Hindi (168), Japanese (1,976), Korean (190), Norwegian (712), Polish (628), Portuguese (1,307), Serbo-Croatian (145), Swedish (561), and Turkish (111).[27]

Some other critically needed languages for Africa and Asia had very few students. Swahili, for example, had 48; Yoruba, 10; Indonesian (Malay), 84; Thai, 98; and Vietnamese, 16. The fact that there was growth in the study of Afro-Asian languages was encouraging. It represented an awareness on the part of American youths of the demands made upon them and their country, and it showed a willingness on their part to help America become better prepared for world leadership.

---

[27] John Harmon, *Modern Foreign Language Enrollments in Colleges and Universities, Fall 1961,* pp. 41–42.

CHAPTER III

Methods and Materials For Teaching Modern Languages

There have been various approaches to modern language learning over the years: grammar-translation, direct (total use of the foreign language), reading, eclectic, and linguistic—to name a few. Sometimes these approaches are called "aims"—for example, the "reading aim." Not a one of these approaches or aims is a method of teaching as such; each represents a theory about language teaching and learning based on a body of knowledge (the language) to be taught. However, the way in which certain theories connected with each approach are applied through instructional procedures in the classroom does cause certain methods to evolve. The techniques of teaching are to achieve certain objectives or aims, and the manner of teaching becomes stylized. Hence, if rapid reading is the aim, there are specific classroom procedures (and out-of-class procedures), and the whole presentation of aspects of language which hasten reading comprehension is labeled the "reading method." If the objective is to translate from the foreign language into English, or from English into the foreign language, based on grammar analysis, then the way of teaching to achieve the translation goals is called the "grammar-translation method." In like manner, each of the other principal approaches to language learning developed regular, systematized instructional techniques in the classroom. The following pages will present the rationale for each new approach (including the new terminology), and will show its practical application through methods of teaching.

Diversity of Methods

Approximately every ten to fifteen years during the first half of the twentieth century a "new" method for improving the teaching of modern foreign languages in American schools appeared. Each new method, championed vigorously by its advocates, focused attention on some aspects of language learning which had been neglected; and it represented dissatisfaction with the methods currently in vogue. Without realizing it completely, proponents of new methods were protesting against the short amount of time allocated in the secondary school and college curriculums for language study— a time interval so short that multiple language skills such as hearing, speaking, reading, writing, and grammar analysis were hard to attain. Those persons who thought that the speaking aim should be paramount stressed the natural, phonetic, or direct method; those who preferred grammar analysis and translating as mental gymnastics for their students stressed the grammar-translation method; the eclectic method sought to combine several methods into one; the reading method was stressed as the only desirable one for most students; the aural-oral method stressed mimicry and memorization; and the audio-lingual method stressed the natural order for arranging the language skills to be learned. There were so many new methods that language teachers and the general public were confused. Each new method was supported by research and evaluation which seemed to prove it to be the best. As a result, the research on certain methods of teaching turned into the teaching of certain methods.

Grammar-Translation

Ancient heritage.   Greek and Latin carried the humanistic traditions of the Western World throughout European educational institutions after the time of the Renaissance. The rediscovery of Greek and Latin literature started a revival of learning, and Latin became the universal language among scholars.

Unfortunately, as time passed, more and more emphasis was placed on verb drills, and noun declensions, an analysis of grammar rules, and on the ways these rules were observed by Greek and Latin writers. The teaching of grammar became an end in itself— a way of "disciplining the mind." Literature, in turn, was dissected so thoroughly on each student's desk as the scholars struggled to parse each sentence, or to translate a few of them into elegant versions of their own language, that much life ebbed out of it on the scholastic operating tables. The classical languages, once so rich in human tradition, carried the tradition with them as they crossed the

Atlantic from Europe to America, but their vitality had decreased in part because of the way they were taught.

Grammar: deductive and inductive. The "old system" of teaching grammar in the United States was deductive or analytical, based on Latin-grammar methods. A grammatical rule would be stated; sentences illustrating the rule came next; then the rule would be applied by translating English sentences into the foreign language, using vocabulary items given in the lesson. This system dominated most foreign language teaching in America from colonial days until well into the twentieth century. The system had much appeal for many students and teachers who were interested in learning to read a foreign language rather than to speak it. It gave them much precise and helpful information, and learning could be tested easily, for example, through objective examinations on verb endings, vocabulary items, or sentences.

The "new system" was inductive or synthetic, and it made its appearance whenever an oral method predominated. After much repetition of pattern drills in phrases or sentences, the grammatical principle was to be induced or inferred by the students, or it was given to them by the teacher.

At the beginning of the twentieth century, the classical languages were usually required for the major professions of law, medicine, pedagogy, and theology. The students of Latin and Greek did not need to speak the foreign languages; they needed to know the syntax of these languages and to be able to translate English sentences into them, or to translate certain classical texts into English. Theological students, for example, might study Greek in order to read portions of the New Testament in the original; but they had no need for speaking Greek. The aim of the classical language teacher was to produce scholars, well trained in grammar rules, who could use their knowledge of these rules in translating to or from the foreign language.

When modern foreign languages became acceptable substitutes for Latin or Greek, the same methods employed by the classicists were used by teachers of the newer languages. The teacher of German or French would drill his students in the rules of grammar (and exceptions), would have the learner recite verb paradigms, and would require a certain number of vocabulary items to be learned from memory for each lesson. The purpose of all this was to prepare the students to turn back into the foreign language certain English sentences which were cleverly devised to illustrate the grammatical principles learned. The grammar-translation method was good mental exercise; the possibilities of talking about grammar were almost limitless.

Direct Method

Even before World War I, people were at work trying to enlarge the scope of modern language teaching. Some of these people were Europeans who insisted that ear training, speaking, reading, and writing should precede grammar analysis. They advocated a "natural" method of learning a language by means of questions and answers on numerous topics. English was strictly forbidden.

A vigorous proponent of a new method was Wilhelm Viëtor, a professor at the University of Marburg, Germany. He championed the use of phonetics in teaching the pronunciation of a foreign language. His ideas were incorporated into the *méthode directe* in France in 1901, into the official modern language teaching method of Germany in 1902, and were brought to America in 1911 by Max Walter, one of Viëtor's students. The four basic principles of the direct method were: [1]

1. Language is made up of sounds, not letters; therefore, speaking should be the first aim. The training of the ear and tongue should precede that of the eye.
2. Connected discourse—not isolated words—should be used, because the expressions given should be full of meaning.
3. Language should be learned in a natural way as a child learns its native language. The grammar-translation method should be discarded.
4. Students should learn grammar inductively.

Language teachers, in principle at least, welcomed the new direct method, which stressed the hearing and speaking objectives first. On the secondary school level, teachers turned eagerly to the teaching of "the living language." These secondary school teachers plunged immediately into the creation of reality in their classrooms.

Oral language, featuring all the sounds, was presented first. Some teachers used phonetic symbols to illustrate sounds, but most served as models for these sounds and asked the students to imitate them.

---

[1] Summarized from Edmond A. Méras, *A Language Teacher's Guide* (New York: Harper & Row, Publishers, 1954), p. 35.

Early lessons were centered around common greetings, learning of numbers, talking about parts of the body, and learning the foreign terms for objects in the classroom. Other series of vocabulary items were added by the use of pictures of fruits, flowers, trees, people, and animals. Maps and posters of foreign countries were used to stimulate additional vocabulary building, as well as to furnish information on aspects of foreign cultures. The visual aids served to give direct comprehension of the vocabulary items presented, and bypassed entirely the use of English. The grammatical structure of the language involved was presented in patterned drills; idioms and verbs were learned through functional use in sentences. Grammar was not "explained"; it was used and learned inductively. Testing was done by oral questions and answers at first. Later, when pupils had learned a sizable amount of vocabulary, written compositions and written answers to questions were given to test mastery of material. Vocabulary items to be tested were often pictures of numerous items with numbers written on them. These items were passed to the pupils, or the latter circulated about the room and jotted down the foreign language term to match the number on the picture. Many of these procedures appealed to the secondary school teacher and pupil alike, but these procedures required much time. College teachers were more conservative in their reception of the direct method. Many welcomed the new approach and emphasized the spoken language in their classes. The vast majority retained the grammar-translation method, yet added the phonetic method to teach pronunciation of sounds. In the college classrooms the phonetic script became another barrier of English-centered explanations set up between the student and the spoken language. Phonetic symbols were talked about, analyzed, and applied to written forms of the language. These symbols constituted another alphabet to be learned before the student proceeded to learning the grammar and translating. Perfect pronunciation of French or German might have been possible through the phonetic method, but the student had little opportunity to speak the language in college classes.

After 1918, when American troops returned from France and World War I, there was increased interest in learning modern languages by the direct method. French and Spanish teachers (German had almost disappeared) in high schools and colleges tried to add more of the language skills to their teaching, beginning with the aural-oral method and continuing through reading, writing, understanding the spoken word, and grammar analysis; but they soon discovered that the amount of time allocated to foreign languages in high schools and colleges was rapidly shrinking as more subjects were competing for time. American education passed through several philosophical changes after 1918. The effects of the swing to "practical" subjects were felt first in high schools, then in colleges and universities. Since the direct method of teaching took more time than was available, a new method came into vogue.

The Eclectic Method

A "common-sense" approach to language learning, called the eclectic method, was brought forth as a realistic compromise. This method was to combine the best of the direct and grammar-translation methods into any presentation which the teacher thought best in view of local circumstances. The chief ways in which the eclectic method operated were as follows:

1. Oral practice of sounds, phonetic drills, speaking of language phrases, and reading aloud were put into the beginning stages of the language course.
2. Questions in the language and answers in the same were used to test comprehension of the spoken language.
3. Audio-visual materials were used to aid vocabulary learning and to give information on the culture of the foreign people.
4. Grammar was explained deductively in order to save time in the classroom.
5. Compositions or sentences were assigned to test the learning of grammar.
6. Translation was still used as the acid test to determine if the student really understood what he had read.

Since correction of written exercises and translation into English of assigned texts took so much of the class time, teachers progressively reduced the amount of oral work until it was of little consequence. Thus, the eclectic method really reverted to the grammar-translation method with some teachers, or to a reading method with others, depending on the interest or capabilities of the individual teacher, or on the local school situation. Teachers became discouraged with the low esteem in which their subjects were held in the secondary schools. The situation called for action.

Reading Method: Its Genesis

American and Canadian committees. In 1924, The Modern Foreign Language Study was launched, sponsored by the Modern Language Association of America, the National Federation of Modern Language Teachers, and other national language groups. This Study, supported by the Carnegie Corporation, was continued nearly seven years, and cost approximately $300,000. It resulted in 18 volumes, 17 covering various aspects of the investigations on the teaching of foreign languages in American and Canadian schools, and the eighteenth containing the *Summary of Reports.* These publications represented much scholarly research by more than sixty American and Canadian language specialists. Many new experiments in modern language teaching were meticulously carried out and the results were published. Cross references were also made to experiments in other academic areas. Thirteen of the 17 numbered volumes, plus *A Summary of Reports on the Modern Foreign Languages,* were published in New York by Macmillan, 1927–1931. Four were published by the University of Toronto Press, one in 1927 (Vol. III), and three in 1928 (Vols. VI, VII, and VIII). The magnitude of The Modern Foreign Language Study appears readily when the numbered volumes are classified according to material treated. However, only a reading of the table of contents of each volume can give an adequate idea of the variety of the investigations undertaken, and the eminence of the collaborators.

Tests: Vol. I, Ben D. Wood, *New York Experiments with Modern Language Tests* (1927); Vol. V, V. A. C. Henmon, *Achievement Tests in the Modern Foreign Languages* (1929); and Vol. XIV, V. A. C. Henmon, *et al., Prognosis Tests in Modern Foreign Languages* (1929).

Administration and enrollments: Vol. IV, C. A. Wheeler, *et al., Enrollment of the Modern Foreign Languages in Secondary Schools and Colleges of the United States* (1928); Vol. VI, Canadian Committee, *Modern Language Instruction in Canada, I* (1928); and Vol. VII, Canadian Committee, *Modern Language Administration in Canada, II* (1928).

Reading: Vol. II, G. T. Buswell, *A Laboratory Study of the Reading of Modern Foreign Languages* (1927).

Word books and idiom lists: Vol. III, M. A. Buchanan, *A Graded Spanish Word Book* (1927); Vol. IX, B. Q. Morgan, *A German Frequency Word Book* (1928); Vol. X, Edward F. Hauch, *A German*

Idiom List, Selected on the Basis of Frequency and Range of Occur rence (1929); Vol. XI, Hayward Keniston, *A Spanish Idiom List, Selected on Basis of Range and Frequency of Occurrence* (1929); Vol. XV, Frederic D. Cheydleur, *French Idiom List, Based on a Running Count of 1,183,000 Words* (1929); and Vol. XVI, George E. Vander Beke, *French Word Book* (1929).

Methodology, teacher training, and teaching: Vol. VIII, M. A. Buchanan, and E. D. MacPhee, *An Annotated Bibliography of Modern Language Methodology* (1928); Vol. XII, Algernon Coleman, *The Teaching of Modern Foreign Languages in the United States* (1929); Vol. XIII, C. M. Purin, *The Training of Teachers of the Modern Foreign Languages* (1929); and Vol. XVII, E. W. Bagster-Collins, *et al., Studies in Modern Language Teaching* (1930).

Apathy toward reports. The Modern Foreign Language Study produced such a wealth of information that it should have elicited numerous appraisals from scholars in the fields of education and foreign languages. But America was riding the soaring spiral of prosperity in 1927, and was in the depths of a depression in 1931; consequently, these publications went almost unnoticed in the American press. Professor Robert Herndon Fife, Chairman of the Committee on Modern Language Teaching, expressed the deep disappointment of the American and Canadian Committee in the following words:

> In the journals of education one finds not infrequently sarcastic observations regarding the futility and one-sidedness of curriculum studies by curriculum specialists, and yet this inquiry, which cost more than three hundred thousand dollars and enjoyed the assistance of sixty-odd collaborators, many of them highly accredited in their department of interest, stirred no one to write an appraisement of its organization and its methods of investigation, or of the reliability of the deductions and interpretations made, or to draw conclusions from the results in terms of the problems of secondary education.[2]

Reading Method: Its Growth

Volume XII of the American and Canadian Committees' report, *The Teaching of Modern Languages in the United States,* prepared

---

[2] Robert Herndon Fife, "A Survey of Tendencies in Modern Language Teaching, 1927–33: Retrospect and Prospect," in Algernon Coleman, *Experiments and Studies in Modern Language Teaching* (Chicago: University of Chicago Press, 1934), p. 2.

by Professor Algernon Coleman, Secretary of the Committee, was published in 1929. Interest focused immediately on the part concerning recommendations on methods. The Committee recommended concentration on an "extensive reading program" in the teaching of modern languages, since it had found that about 87 per cent of the secondary school pupils enrolled in a foreign language studied the language for only two years. The reading skill seemed to be the most feasible of attainment in so short a time. Modern language teachers rushed to endorse or to attack "The Coleman Report," but they now had a new path to follow: the reading method. Professor Fife summed up the language teachers' interest in the new method as follows:

> No one who has attended teachers' meetings or read the contributions in journals devoted to any curriculum subject need feel surprised at this concentration of interest. Particularly in the foreign-language field, method has always been a fetish, and no religious fundamentalist ever pointed out the single, narrow path leading to salvation with more zeal than the modern-language teacher the particular formulas by which he seeks to lead his students to achievement.[3]

Experiments in the reading of English showed that quantity of reading by a pupil had a marked effect on the quality of his achievement and comprehension. Also, the faster a pupil read, the better he understood, according to tests and experiments. Statistical data from some experiments in the modern language field, supported by the American Council reading tests, indicated that the same acceleration in rate of reading and in comprehension would result in modern languages (as it had in English), if the amount of reading were sharply increased. Language teachers seized upon word and idiom lists and had their students learn the 1,500 most frequently used words in the languages being studied. By learning the basic list of 1,500 words, a student was supposed to be able to read without too much trouble most of the literary works assigned to him. Writers and publishers of textbooks busily turned out new texts for class use, being careful to use the "graded" approach to reading. A "direct-reading" method was developed by one writer; another published a "cognate approach" to reading.

---

[3] *Ibid.,* pp. 2–3.

Characteristics of reading method. The reading method had the following characteristics:

1. Pronunciation was stressed at first, because even in silent reading a person's mind might tend to suggest sounds for the words in the text.
2. Grammar was taught for recognition only.
3. Oral use of the foreign language in the classroom was restricted usually to pronunciation drills and a few questions in the foreign language to test comprehension of materials read.
4. Translation from English to the foreign language was usually omitted.
5. Reading materials introduced words and idioms at a predetermined rate, and were based on the scientifically prepared word and idiom lists.
6. Materials written by foreign authors were rewritten, where necessary, to restrict the selections to the graded vocabulary level desired.

As an aftermath of the Coleman Report, modern foreign language teachers seemed to accept the inevitability of the two-year interval allocated for their work, and limited their efforts to teaching reading. Reading was the "surrender value" of two years of language study, and the two years given to languages in the secondary schools were shoved back toward the end of the high school period to grades 11 and 12. Even in the late 1950's, it was almost impossible in many schools for a pupil to begin language study in grade 10.

Students, teachers, and school administrators were dissatisfied with the limitations of the reading method, but the educational climate was not yet right for the language teachers to ask for more time in order to develop more of the language skills in their pupils. American secondary school curriculums had become more and more antitraditional. Studies were made of drop-outs in the high schools, and content subjects were blamed. New "life-adjustment" courses could not be added, if foreign languages were retained. If some parents and pupils insisted on having foreign languages in the curriculum, these persons might be offered "general language" or world literature in English translation, instead.

This anti-foreign language attitude was reflected on many levels: The American Youth Commission's report, *What the High Schools Ought to Teach* (1940); The National Education Association's Educational Policies Commission's book, *Education for All American Youth* (1944), Harvard University's *General Education in a Free Society* (1945), and the U.S. Office of Education's Program of "Life-Adjustment Education" (1946).

The "Harvard Report" of 1945, as *General Education in a Free Society* was familiarly called, was widely discussed in college and university circles and at meetings of secondary school superintendents. The twelve Harvard professors and their consultants who prepared the Report recommended a "core-curriculum" for the secondary schools, but foreign language study was not part of the core. The few gifted children who could profit from it should have language study; it would contribute toward improving their command of English, through carefully prepared translations. Foreign literature in English translation, however, was more profitable for most of the students, according to the Report.

General Language. Since the Harvard Report specifically recommended General Language as a substitute for foreign languages in the program of studies for the less able secondary school students, many schools in several states initiated orientation courses to the study of one or more languages, to the cultures represented by these languages, or to the story of language origins. The General Language course was usually offered in junior high school as an "exploratory" course in language learning.

A United States Office of Education survey in the fall of 1959 revealed by type of school the extent to which General Language courses continued to be taught in American public secondary schools. About 80 per cent of the schools teaching General Language offered it in the eighth grade; about 14 per cent, in the seventh grade; and approximately six per cent, in the ninth grade. The number of schools which offered General Language constituted 1.3 per cent of all public secondary schools and 1.9 per cent of all schools which taught foreign languages. In over 93 per cent of the schools which offered General Language, foreign languages were also taught.[4]

The Harvard Report had detrimental effects on language study in the general education program of colleges. From 1947 until 1953, the per cents of modern foreign language enrollment dropped annually in colleges. Language requirements for entrance to college were abandoned by a large number of institutions, and 46 of them dropped the foreign language requirement for the B.A. degree

---

[4] Esther M. Eaton, *Foreign Languages in Public Secondary Schools: Interim Report* (Washington, D.C.: United States Government Printing Office, 1963), p. 25.

during the interval 1947–53. Many teachers colleges never had a language requirement for graduation; others reduced their requirement from two years of study to one, then abolished the requirement completely. Teacher trainees were going to teach "core" subjects; therefore, they did not need to bother to learn a foreign language. "Opinionnaires," circulated among secondary school superintendents, showed that these future employers of teachers were in favor of having teachers colleges drop the foreign language requirement. It was impossible, the argument went, to know which foreign language would be needed by a person. If he studied French, he might need German; if he studied German, he might need Spanish. It was useless, therefore, to study a foreign language. English was sufficient.

But English was not enough for millions of Americans in the 1940's. While many educators were attacking the poor results in foreign language teaching and were dropping foreign languages from the schools, America's Armed Forces in Europe and Asia were experiencing a desperate need for knowledge of other languages in their effort to conquer and occupy enemy territories. The reading method of the 1930's had produced a generation of literate (but inarticulate) Americans, and the Armed Services needed officers and enlisted men who could speak the languages of their allies as well as those of their enemies. The speaking had to be natural, authentic, and fluent. So out of war-time needs arose a new method which was to have a revitalizing effect upon language pedagogy in the United States—the so-called "Army method." (This new method will be discussed in chronological context with some other language programs of the Armed Services, because the "Army method" used some of the techniques which had been developed in earlier programs.)

Vanguard of the Army Method

The Army's new, dynamic, much publicized language method had many less publicized contributors: cultural anthropologists and descriptive linguists, American Council of Learned Societies, college professors, Navy's Japanese Language School, Army Air Force Language School, and Inter-American Training Center, to mention the principal ones.

Cultural anthropologists and linguists. The new techniques of linguistic science, applied in the drill sessions of the Armed Forces language schools, were outgrowths of knowledge gained by cultural anthropologists and linguists in their study of North American Indian dialects. The anthropologists considered language as a stream of sounds, systematically arranged or patterned, by means of which human beings in a given culture could communicate with each other. Many of these anthropologists also were linguists who found that clusters of sounds could be analyzed and described. These linguists discovered that there was a great deal of difference between the spoken language and the written one in cultures which had both. They pointed out that in all cultures most people in a given community had learned to speak their native language, but that many of these could not read or write it. The written symbols, therefore, were not the "essence of language"; the patterned groups of sounds (the vocal symbols) were.

The descriptive linguists broke down a language in terms of its utterances (sounds), first making a complete phonemic transcription of the utterances to show the clusters of sounds and the type of juncture (pause) between the clusters. Thus, the linguists could filter out groups of sounds and treat them as separate units. The two requisites for this living language study were (1) a native speaker of the language to be learned, and (2) a trained linguist who could separate out, phonemically, the patterned structure of the language. Through a descriptive analysis of the sounds and sound system of a language (the phonology), the linguist could note the functions of inflections and of forms derived from the basic sounds (the morphology), as well as the orderly arrangement of these sound groups and their mutual relationship in the complete speech utterance (the syntax).

American Council of Learned Societies. The American Council of Learned Societies, supported by Rockefeller Foundation funds, had already set up in the fall of 1942 an intensive language program in 18 universities and colleges. This program, based on linguistic science, was under the direction of Mortimer Graves, Administrative Secretary of the ACLS, aided by J. Milton Cowan. Army curriculum planners believed that the new teaching techniques sponsored by the American Council of Learned Societies might be more suitable for an intensive language program than the traditional language pedagogy; they therefore engaged linguists of the ACLS to prepare and direct much of the initial work.

The Navy's Japanese Language School.[5]   The Navy was first to build a language program. Some of the curricular changes incorporated into the Army language program were taken from the Navy's Japanese Language School, which started on October 1, 1941, at Harvard University and the University of California. The Navy's language program was intensive, with eighteen contact hours with the language each week. It was designed to give the students fluency in Japanese within twelve months time. The objective was fourfold: speaking, understanding, reading, and writing.

Reading aloud was the basis of oral drill, and the Navy adopted the graded readers especially prepared by Naol Naganuma of Tokyo. A supply of these readers came from Japan in September, 1941. Japanese was used exclusively after the third week. Qualified teachers, rather than informants, were the drill masters, and classes were limited to four or five students. Pronunciation and language structure were taught by mimicry and memorization. The Navy's program did not put so much stress on the area's contemporary history, institutions, and geography as did the Army's. The primary need of the Navy was for officer-trainees who could work in Intelligence: translate captured Japanese reports of field orders, intercept messages, question prisoners of war, broadcast in Japanese, and interpret.

The Navy later changed the name of its school to Navy Oriental Language School and added Chinese and other Oriental languages. Later, some of the languages of Western Europe were added, and in 1946 all of the Navy's language schools were transferred to Washington. The Navy's Japanese Language School was successful because of the careful planning of curriculum content, careful lesson plans of the course hour by hour, and rigorous supervision of the teachers and their teaching technique.

In addition to the Japanese Language School, the Navy established two Schools of Military Government, one at Columbia University (June 17, 1942), and the other at Princeton University (October 3, 1944). These language schools emphasized (1) oral Japanese and Melanesian Pidgin English, (2) the study of native customs, (3) native and colonial governmental institutions, and (4) some technical aspects of military government itself.[6] In these two

---

[5] Robert John Matthew, *Language and Area Studies in the Armed Services* (Washington, D.C.: American Council on Education, 1947), pp. 14–24.
[6] *Ibid.,* p. 28.

schools, a total of 1,412 men were trained. The Navy found it possible to teach students a foreign language in a short time. It also discovered that "training in government and administration is not the exclusive prerogative of any one discipline, but is instead a grouping of disciplines cutting across both departmental and faculty lines." [7]

Army Air Force program. The conversational approach to the teaching of Spanish and Portuguese was begun in 1941 by the United States Army Air Force, under the auspices of the Works Projects Administration. General Henry Arnold initiated the program when a group of 100 picked officers were ordered to learn Spanish. Henry Besso and Solomon Lipp of New York City, employed by the Works Project Administration, were engaged to teach these officers. The instructors developed the textbook *Conversational Spanish for the Army Air Forces of the United States,* which was also used by the Navy. The Works Project Administration trained other teachers in the conversational method and sent them to different parts of the United States where language courses were being established.

Inter-American Training Center. In June, 1942, the Inter-American Training Center was organized by the Office of the Coordinator of Inter-American Affairs and administered by the American Council of Learned Societies. Dean Henry Grattan Doyle of George Washington University was appointed Director of the Washington Center. Although the Inter-American Training Center lasted only through June, 1944, in the two years of its existence it gave intensive oral training in Spanish and Portuguese.

The Army Method

The Japanese attack on Pearl Harbor on December 7, 1941, touched off a gigantic United States war effort which sent American armed forces to fight in North Africa, Europe, Asia, and the islands of the Pacific. Before the Japanese attack, as early as November 1, 1941, the Army had set up a Military Intelligence Service Language School at the Presidio in San Francisco to train 60 Americans of Japanese ancestry (Nisei) as translators and interpreters. A staff of

---

[7] *Ibid.*

four officers gave these trainees basic Japanese and training in military Japanese. After the outbreak of war with Japan, the school was moved to Camp Savage, Minnesota. In November, 1942, the War Department set up a one-year course in Japanese for Caucasians at the University of Michigan, where the first class started on January 5, 1943, with 21 instructors and 150 trainees.

Army Specialized Training Program. By December 1942, the Army, well aware of its need for language and area specialists who could help conquer and later occupy and govern enemy territories, created the Army Specialized Training Program (ASTP) and its Foreign Area and Language Study Curriculum. The new program began in April, 1943.

The ASTP stressed language and area studies, especially the contemporary history, social institutions, geographical aspects of the region, and the everyday life of its people. The program's general objectives and detailed content had been formulated at a conference held April 16–18, 1943, at the School of Military Government in Charlottesville, Virginia, and were based on an outline prepared by the Office of the Provost Marshal General. The curriculum consisted of three divisions: [8]

1. *Special knowledge of characteristics and conditions of areas of occupation.* Such knowledge included detailed information about (a) the physical geography of the area, (b) its people, (c) their means of livelihood, (d) the government of the area, (e) the mores of the people, and (f) the historical background and contemporary world affairs.

2. *Language training.* The principal languages taught were French, German, Italian, Japanese, Malay, and Melanesian Pidgin. Further language training was given to officers who already had speaking or reading ability in a foreign language useful to the area to which they were assigned. Other officers were given instruction in one of the area's major languages. All instruction was of an intensive nature, making use of native speakers (informants) whenever possible. Seventeen contact hours of study were provided each week, one hour five days per week for demonstrations by senior instructors of the structure of the language, and two hours of drill six days a week with native speakers of the language. The number

---

[8] Summarized from Matthew, *Language and Area Studies in the Armed Services,* pp. 58–63.

of trainees in each drill session was limited to ten, and the average program lasted for nine months.

3. *Special application of civilian specialties to military government situations.* To ensure that officer-trainees would appreciate the condition of their respective sciences, professions, or specialties in the area for which they were being prepared, and to give them practice in fitting their special competencies into a comprehensive plan for the area concerned, specific problems would be assigned to designated teams of officers. The latter, in consultation with faculty members who had competence in various fields of technical or professional specialization, would work toward solving the problems. These officer-trainees lived together and used the foreign language whenever possible.

Unusual features of the Army method. An analysis of the Army's method of teaching languages reveals the following distinctive educational features:

1. *Maximum course content in minimum time.* The 17 hours of contact with a language each week over a period of 36 weeks gave the trainees 612 hours of instruction and drill, or approximately five times as much as they would have had in the usual college language class during an academic year.

2. *High standards of student selection and performance.* Students were carefully screened for the language work, and high standards of achievement were demanded. Only 29 per cent of the trainees who went to the end of their term were graduated .

3. *Superb motivation.* A trainee in the ASTP tried to succeed in order to remain in an interesting, self-improving situation. Furthermore, he was motivated by patriotism. He could help his country's war effort better by preparing himself to serve in foreign lands.

4. *Integration of area studies with language.* In addition to the 17 contact hours in language per week, the trainees might have up to 10 hours of work in the history, politics, geography, or economics of the area. This extra work brought several other disciplines to bear upon their training in an interdepartmental cooperative organization.

5. *Objectives were clearly defined.* The Army wanted its trainees to have a command of the colloquial spoken form of the language to the point of speaking fluently, accurately, and with an acceptable

approximation to a native pronunciation; and almost perfect auditory comprehension of the language as spoken by a native.

6. *Classes were small.* Army language classes were limited to 10 students to each instructor.

Results of the Army method. The success of the Army's language schools was amazing to an American public accustomed to hearing the statement that Americans could not learn a foreign language. The program was less than six months old when newspapers and magazines began to publicize its success. Unfortunately, many of the accounts were exaggerated and biased. The Army by some superior, magic formula had taught its men to speak a foreign language in three months; the Army could teach languages better than teachers in high schools and colleges, so wrote the journalists. What the newspapers failed to say was that on 227 college campuses, 55 of which had the language and area schools, the language programs were usually under the direction of college professors. These professional language teachers, fluent speakers of the languages they taught, were assisted by native speakers. But to use the Army method, the teachers had to be trained linguists in order to analyze the natives' speech, because the learning was based upon this analysis.

A quick glance at the indexes of language journals (*French Review, Italica, German Quarterly, Hispania, Modern Language Journal,* and *PMLA*) published from 1944 to 1946 will show what an impact the Army method had upon college teachers and what implications they saw in it for the future of language teaching in America.[9] Also, many other educational journals published similar articles. Most of these writers endorsed the validity of an oral approach to language learning; some showed that reading and writing came easier when the student had a solid oral command of the language. Other articles pointed out the added educational gains of concentrating on an area and its language in a combined program. Some of the writers were critical, pointing out that the educational goals of colleges and universities were so different from those of the Army that the intensive language program did not fit into the pattern of higher education. Furthermore, the detractors wrote, many soldiers who had learned to speak a foreign language in a

---

[9] See Maxim Newmark, *Twentieth Century Modern Language Teaching* (New York: Philosophical Library, 1948), for reprints of the principal articles.

short time had also forgotten the language about as fast, if they had had no chance to use it.

But the Army method had excited the general public; [10] it had been interesting and satisfying to its own students; it did influence postwar language teaching in high schools and colleges. It showed that Americans were quite proficient in language learning if given proper motivation, a longer period for study, well-trained teachers, and an intensive approach. A few colleges were able to establish intensive language programs, but American educators in the late 1940's were still hostile toward languages. Many good features of the Army method had to languish for about ten years before they were revived in the "new," audio-lingual method. The Army established its permanent Language School at Monterey, California, in 1946.

The Audio-Lingual Approach: Language in the New Key

Language for communication became the dominant emphasis after 1953 in the new American method of teaching modern foreign languages. Taking its cue from the success of the Army method, this new technique stressed a natural order in teaching the language skills: a progression from listening to foreign language speech patterns, to active speaking, reading, and writing. It stressed that language learning was a process of forming certain speech habits, and that there should be a maximum of structural pattern learning and a minimum of isolated word study and grammar analysis. Because the Army method's terminology "aural-oral" (based on "mim-mem" —mimicry and memorization), conveyed almost identical sounds to the listener and unclear meaning to the reader, language specialists in the late 1950's began to use a new term—"audio-lingual." Among the active sponsors of this new phrase were Nelson Brooks of Yale University and Mary Thompson of the Glastonbury, Connecticut, schools, who used the term often in public addresses and in later published works.[11] George Winchester Stone, Jr., Executive Secretary of the Modern Language Association (1956–63), coined the

---

10 See Matthew, *Language and Area Studies in the Armed Services*, pp. 188–210, for an extensive bibliography.

11 See Nelson Brooks, *Language and Language Learning* (New York: Harcourt, Brace & World, Inc., 1960), and Chapter V of the present monograph.

term "new key" in 1956, adding it as a descriptive label for the new approach.[12]

Listening, speaking, reading, and writing are ascending notes in the "new key," representing a new sequence in language learning. In the traditional presentation of language skills, reading and writing had been placed ahead of understanding and speaking.

Briefly stated, the philosophy underlying the audio-lingual approach is as follows:

Language is essentially sound; it consists of human oral communication. Graphic symbols are inadequate for representing the many nuances of the spoken tongue. In fact, language is not primarily the written form but the spoken, everyday language of the ordinary person. It is usually conversation carried on between two or more people.

Hence, in teaching a foreign language, much practice in hearing and speaking should come first. Reading and writing follow after the basic speech patterns of the language have been acquired. These are learned through memorized dialogues dealing with everyday situations. Grammar is learned incidentally through constant practice of "structures" occurring in the dialogues. These structures are not graded or classified; grammar points are learned as they occur in the course of the conversation. The conversation is not constructed, slowed up, or made easy. From the beginning the student hears the natural speech—preferably of a native—at normal speed. the learner hears and imitates. He is asked to repeat meticulously the model he listens to; he is not to construct original sentences. Answers to questions are cued. Thus the possibility of error is practically excluded.

In view of the emphasis on hearing and speaking, the use of electrophonic devices is invaluable. The tape recorder and the language laboratory contribute greatly to the efficacy of the new method.

Culture, which is concerned primarily with the everyday habits and customs of the foreign people, should come through the language of which it forms an essential part. "Refinement culture"—facts about the history, art, music and literature of the foreign people—will come later through reading. Since the aim is to make

---

12 The idea for the term may have come from Susanne K. Langer's *Philosophy in a New Key* (Cambridge, Mass.: Harvard University Press, 1942).

the learner bilingual, the foreign language classroom should be a cultural isle. English is practically excluded.

Methodology

Listening with a purpose. Borrowing from the Army method's use of linguistic science, the audio-lingual approach treats a new language as a system of sounds, and the student begins his study of the language by listening to these sounds as they are given repeatedly in meaningful phrases and at normal speed. Much use is made of records or magnetic tapes on which the voices of native speakers repeat these phrases into the student's ears. Ear training (the audio part of the method), is the major activity at first. The period devoted solely to listening varies in length with the teacher and with the age level of the class. No written language accompanies the early stages of ear training; training through the eyes comes later.

Many secondary school and college students approach the learning of a modern foreign language with ears which have not been conditioned to listen acutely and with minds which give passive attention to sounds. Often these students have turned on radios or television sets while "studying" or have played phonograph records as "background" for homework. Misuse of mass media of communication over a period of years has contributed to a state in which ears do not hear the sounds (or noises) which are bombarding them from all directions in their own culture. As a result, it is very necessary now to begin a new language by training the students' ears to listen carefully and with a purpose.

Teachers give ear training to students in the classroom by using the foreign language from the very beginning. Students hear the sounds relating to greetings, farewells, a person's name, parts of the body, inquiries about health and climate, and the usual sounds connected with the names of classroom objects. Students begin to associate these sounds with meaning; and to show that they understand the sounds, they respond at first to simple commands in a nonverbal manner by pointing or by doing what the teacher asks them to do. The response is by the group, or part of it, or by an individual, according to the teacher's direction.

Verbal responses to simple questions or commands are encouraged just as soon as the students have learned the sounds, have connected meaning with them, and are familiar with the intonation (sing-song pattern) which accompanies them. Later, further exercises in ear training for practice in understanding are given through relating well-known tales, anecdotes, poems, or selections already read, or through songs in the foreign language.

Speaking according to plan. Listening for understanding is followed soon by speaking, the two skills being interdependent. After he has listened to the language phrases numerous times, the student begins repeating them; he imitates his teacher-model, or the patterns of sound which he hears on tape or disk. At the beginning, the teacher plays the triple role of model, judge, and manager.[13] Not only does the teacher need to possess almost native ability to model the sounds with the accompanying accuracy of intonational patterns, but he also has to be able to judge the accuracy of the pupil's imitation, and serve as a manager who can give the pupil enough oral drill practice to ensure that the ears and tongue are trained properly.

Systematic practice in speaking is centered around carefully prepared dialogues (built around real-life situations), in which new vocabulary, idioms, language structure (grammar), and cultural materials of daily life are introduced. Dialogue adaptations (structure drills) in the classroom or in the language laboratory "reinforce" the learning of materials already presented. The students memorize the basic dialogues exactly as they are given on disks or tapes, after the teacher has made the dialogue situation and phrases absolutely clear by going through each dialogue once, section by section, and by dramatizing appropriate parts of it. The English explanations of the dialogue are not translations unless they are necessary for comprehension. Normal speed in the foreign language is maintained from the beginning, and students are asked to dramatize the real-life situations with other students.

Many types of pattern drills can be formed from a well-constructed dialogue to bring out language structures, verb conjugations, vocabulary items, and idiomatic expressions. The following are common types of drills: (1) *repetition,* in which items such as verb forms or object pronouns are repeated so often that the student

---

[13] See Patricia O'Connor, *Modern Foreign Languages in High School: Prereading Instruction,* Bulletin 1960, No. 9 (Washington, D.C.: Government Printing Office, 1960).

learns them correctly; (2) *transformation,* where one item may be changed to another, as single items to plural, positives to negatives, questions to answers; (3) *substitution,* in which one item can be substituted for another, such as demonstrative adjectives for definite articles; (4) *integration,* in which two independent clauses may be combined; (5) *expansion,* which enlarges a sentence by the inclusion of a word or words; and (6) *contraction,* which shortens the phrase by omitting a word or words.[14]

All pattern drills at first are presented orally; later the students are allowed to see them while they practice variations upon them. Still later, students are asked to read aloud former dialogues which they have learned.

Reading. After several weeks of listening to and repeating structural language patterns given in dialogue form, the student is introduced to reading. At first, the reading materials are those same dialogues and drill exercises which he has practiced speaking. The early reading serves for oral practice (reading aloud) as was done in the Armed Services language schools. At this point, the student can usually read anything which he has experienced through the previous audio-lingual practice. He already knows that the language sounds have a system of order and a system of form. The written symbols for these sounds, although inadequate representations of them, serve to add a visual dimension which reinforces those of hearing and speaking. Progressing from the simple, controlled vocabulary of the early mimicry-memorization exercises, the student gradually acquires a wider vocabulary through reading carefully graded textbooks.

Reading is of three types: intensive, extensive, and supplementary. Intensive reading is usually that of the classroom, limited in scope at first to materials already learned through oral practice, and directed carefully by the teacher. The purpose of such reading is to increase knowledge of vocabulary, idioms, and language structures, preparing the way for the second stage. Extensive reading is quantitative in nature, allowing the student more independence to pursue his own interests over a wide range of possible fields. He reads

---

[14] For excellent helps on dialogue construction and on the use of pattern drills, see the New York State language syllabi, Remunda Cadoux, general ed., *French for Secondary Schools, German for Secondary Schools,* and *Spanish for Secondary Schools* (Albany, N.Y.: New York State Education Department, 1960–61).

materials which are in keeping with his ability and which give him a sense of pleasure and accomplishment. Supplementary reading consists of additional materials assigned to the intensive and extensive lists. These readings are chosen to give specific information on some aspect of the culture of the foreign country whose language is being studied.

In the transition from the audio-lingual period to that of visual presentation of written words, the recommended technique is (1) to have the students repeat the dialogue orally several times before they see the printed text, (2) to have them repeat the dialogue orally several more times with the text in front of them, (3) to have them read the dialogue silently from the text, (4) to have them read the whole dialogue in chorus, imitating the way the teacher divides the sentence into phonetic groups, and (5) to have certain individual students read portions of the dialogue aloud.

When new materials are assigned for intensive reading, the teacher's role is (1) to motivate the students' interest in the selection chosen, (2) to eliminate many of the difficulties by giving definitions, synonyms, or antonyms for unfamiliar words or idioms, (3) to emphasize certain allusions to cultural practices, (4) to relate the theme of the story, if possible, to the students' experiences or needs, (5) to have the students read the passage silently, and (6) to check the students' comprehension of the story content by asking them questions based on it.

Extensive reading is usually done silently in the classroom or in the students' homes. The students make selection from lists posted by the teacher. The teacher tries to motivate certain readings in conformity with known student interests or abilities, and gives all the other helps mentioned under the intensive reading techniques. The extensive reading is meant to increase the students' skill (speed) in reading for comprehension, and to give them a rapidly expanding passive vocabulary.

Supplementary reading is done in English during the prereading, audio-lingual weeks of beginning language study. Later, these readings are assigned in English or in the foreign language. The supplementary materials are chosen to stimulate the students' interest in the foreign country and its total culture, and to increase their desire to read more about it.

Writing. After much listening, speaking, and reading aloud, the student takes the last important step to writing. New-key writing is a graduated process, going from *controlled* writing and composition to *directed* composition, and finally to *free* composition. At first, the controlled writing is usually the copying of sentences from some of the dialogues learned earlier; it often is "writing" from dictation some specific patterned drills previously learned. This early writing also serves to reinforce the student's memory by adding hand training to that of ear, tongue, and eye. Early writing is always within the framework of what the student has already practiced, and the purpose is to ensure mastery of the earlier audio-lingual materials.

Later, writing is expanded by having the student rewrite a dialogue between two boys, for example, to one between two girls. The student is directed to change tenses or persons in a model paragraph and rewrite the whole. Brief composition based on a given vocabulary follows later. These brief compositions, like all previous exercises in writing, are guided by the teacher at all times. The emphasis is always on complete and correct learning of meaningful phrases already experienced in the foreign language, never on the jigsaw-puzzle technique of fitting phrases together to illustrate rules of grammer. Grammar analysis as such is postponed until a much later stage.

In directed composition the students have to follow certain directions which the teacher gives them. The teacher might give such directions as "Write a letter to a friend. Ask him what his plans are for the summer. Tell him that you plan to go to Europe with a group of students led by your language teacher. Ask your friend if he can go with you."

Free composition comes after the students have a good stock of vocabulary items, a mastery of grammar structures, and an ability to organize ideas in an original, independent manner. It serves as a good evaluation of the students' academic progress in two respects: (1) It gives the teacher a clear idea of the amount and accuracy of language learning which has taken place. (2) It also indicates the over-all ability of the student to present his ideas in organized form. The free compositions help to give students greater ability to think in the foreign language, as well as a feeling for style.

Old Notes in the New Key

The audio-lingual approach is not new in regard to its essential aims (teaching of the basic language skills), nor in its arrangement of these skills, nor in its use of linguistic science. Its newness is one of emphasis and direction—the application to peace-time teaching of the successful aural-oral techniques used by the Armed Services during World War II, and the creation of new teaching materials. It is a turning away from the traditional classroom procedure (which has been grammar-translation centered) to an active use of the foreign language as an authentic manifestation of the foreign culture. It is another twentieth-century renewal of the oral method, with emphasis on language for communication.

Oral method.   Listening and speaking, primary language skills in the new key, are very old notes indeed, going back in methodology to the German Reform Movement at the beginning of the twentieth century. The philosophy that the audio-lingual approach is the correct way to begin language study has been expressed many times before.

Harold E. Palmer in his book *The Oral Method of Teaching Languages* [15] quotes Johann Wolfgang von Goethe's statement (eighteenth century) from *Aus meinem Leben* on the way he learned languages:

> Thus I had learned Latin, just like German, French, English, only through practice, without rule and without system . . . everything seemed to come naturally to me. I retained the words, their formations and transformations in my ear and in my mind, and I employed the language with ease for writing and talking.

Palmer also quotes the following statement from Arthur Powell's article, "The Teaching of English to Foreigners," in *The Modern Language Quarterly,* October, 1904: "I think . . . it is an immense gain if no book comes between the teacher and the class, and if the teaching is oral or nearly so." [16]

About the time when the reading method was in full vogue, an unsigned article entitled, "Ten Axioms Governing the Main Principles to be Observed in the Teaching and Learning of Foreign Lan-

---

[15] Harold E. Palmer, *The Oral Method of Teaching Languages* (New York: Harcourt, Brace & World, Inc., 1926), p. 4.
[16] *Ibid.*

guages," appeared in the *Bulletin of the Institute for Research in English Teaching* (Japan), No. 101 (February, 1934), pp. 4–8. The ten axioms given are true progenitors of much of the audio-lingual methodology: (1) Language consists essentially of linguistic symbols. (2) A language may be looked upon as both a "code" and "as speech." (3) The learning of a language consists in coming to know the meanings of a sufficient number of these symbols and to associate them with meaning. (4) From the viewpoint of linguistic methodology, the learning of a language consists in developing a number of primary and secondary skills. (5) Hearing and speaking what is heard are among primary skills. (6) Reading and writing are among secondary skills. (7) Translation is a secondary skill. (8) Pronunciation is an integral part of a language, concerned with sounds of the language and their distribution. (9) Grammar is an integral part of the language and reflects canons of usage. (10) The thorough acquisition of a small vocabulary is the best equipment for coming to acquire a larger vocabulary.[17]

Culture. Study of culture is another old note played in the new key. Films and filmstrips which reproduce scenes and sounds from the land whose language is being studied help the student to know and to respect the culture of other people.

The audio-lingual approach tends to emphasize the anthropological concept of culture (the everyday patterns of social conduct), rather than the traditional, humanistic viewpoint (art, literature, music, philosophy, religion). Two aspects of the audio-lingual methodology foster the anthropological concept: the dialogues, and the extensive reading materials. In the dialogues it is natural for people to talk about meals, movies, popular music, marriage, shopping, sidewalk cafés, and the like. In their extensive readings, students usually read newspapers and magazines rather than literary masterpieces, when they are given free choice. Much practical information about contemporary life in the foreign country is thus conveyed interestingly to young students through these channels, thus adding the concept of area to that of language. This presentation of culture has the merit of being more objective and less indoc-

---

[17] Summarized from Algernon Coleman, *An Analytical Bibliography of Modern Language Teaching*, Vol. 2 (Chicago: The University of Chicago Press, 1938), p. 45.

trinating than had been some of the earlier, stereotyped presentations.

However, the audio-lingual drills, plus intensive and extensive readings, leave very little time for supplementary readings, and most of the students cannot add much depth to their study of the history, literature, economic geography, politics, fine arts, and folklore of the area. Language teachers seem to be coming to the opinion that the anthropological concept of culture should be presented in the dialogues, but that the humanistic aspects should be introduced consistently in the reading assignments.

Extensive reading. In the 1930's, advocates of the reading method had stressed the importance of much fast reading for comprehension, for vocabulary building, and for cultural information. The approach to the reading goal thirty years ago was by way of word-frequency lists, simplified texts, and standardized tests. One has only to turn to Algernon Coleman's *Experiments and Studies in Modern Language Teaching,*[18] a compilation for the Committee on Modern Language Teaching, to become aware of the value of extensive reading. Michael West's *Bilingualism* (1924) and *Learning to Read a Foreign Language* (1926) gave convincing testimony to the effectiveness of his reading method. He adapted the language (English) which he was teaching to the age level of his Bengali pupils. New-key teaching advocates similar adaptation to age level; the new-key students, however, usually do not read as widely from literature, biography, folklore, fables, and legends as did students under the old-key method.

Grammar. Another old note used is grammar, but it is cleverly disguised as "prescripts," "statements," "systematic summaries," or "rules-of-thumb." The big difference between new-key teaching and the traditional is that these "summaries" are given to the students as a kind of reference after they have already learned the language patterns which are covered in the summaries. One other difference in presentation of grammar is that the use of English is taboo. Explanations of grammar principles in English are thought to be detrimental to the student's progress in the foreign language. Grammar principles are given in the structural drills, and the student is supposed to be able to infer what the usages are. A clear statement

---

[18] Algernon Coleman, *Experiments and Studies in Modern Language Teaching* (Chicago: University of Chicago Press, 1934), pp. 100–144.

of a grammatical rule, however, often helps to speed up the acquisition of more language, because it brings a sense of order. The omission of English explanations in the audio-lingual approach is a fad, or a personal idiosyncrasy on the part of the teacher, and does not necessarily represent the best way to teach.

Vincenzo Cioffari, in an article on grammar, summed up the use of English in teaching grammar as follows:

> The exclusive use of any one approach means incomplete teaching. Suppose, for example, one uses only the reading approach. That part of language which is based on sounds and that part of meaning which depends on those sounds is lost or impaired. Suppose one uses only the oral approach, to the exclusion of grammatical patterns. That part of language which is based on structure will be impaired, and the student will never develop the ability for self-expression. He will be limited to the exact repetition of set phrases. Suppose one uses only the direct method, to the exclusion of explanations in the native language. In the first place the student will be limited in his words and actions and in the second place he will be bewildered by the new language which hovers about him meaninglessly. If a simple sentence in English can clarify a whole day's work, it is wasteful not to take advantage of it and speed right along. There is still no substitute for common sense.[19]

Translation. Only in advanced stages of new-key methodology is translation used. Its special purpose is to relate two languages which are already well-known to the student, and to have him comment on what is gained, lost, or changed in translating from the foreign language to English. Translation is not used as a word-for-word "matching" game. The audio-lingual method's handling of translation gives the student an increased appreciation of the foreign language he is studying, as well as more respect for his own.

Linguistics. Linguistics, the scientific study of language, is an old note which came into the new key from its successful application in the Army's language schools. At first, it came loaded with so much technical jargon that it often was more confusing than helpful to teachers. Without reference to meaning, structural linguists classified the phonetic elements of a language (the noises people make when they speak) into contrasting units of pattern called *phonemes,* which were stated to be classes of elements called *allo-*

---

[19] Vincenzo Cioffari, "Grammar—Beware!" *The Modern Language Journal,* XLII (October, 1958), pp. 284–87.

phones. Upon analyzing the language sounds, linguists found phonemes to be in complementary distribution, similar phonetically, and occurring in congruent patterns. This systematizing of the set of noises people make in a language was called *phonemics.* Recurring patterned elements of one or more phonemes were called *morphemes; morphology* was the study of word formation; *lexicology,* the study of lists of morphemes; and *syntax,* the study of constructions into which words could be placed. Therefore, the descriptive grammar of a language consisted in its *phonology* (phonetics and phonemics) and its structural principles, *morphemics* (morphophonemics, arrangement, morphology, syntax, and lexicology).

Later, when the structural linguists started talking to laymen in less technical terms, and when they illustrated linguistic principles through their practical application to the teaching of a specific language, modern foreign language teachers found valuable allies in the linguistic scientists.

Applied linguistics aids language teachers in two general respects: in methodology, and in materials for classroom use. In methodology, the linguists stress that speech is the primary consideration and writing, the secondary. To learn speech, people must develop certain automatic-response habits. Most of the classroom time at first, according to the linguists, should be spent in choral or individual repetition of pattern practices and of carefully prepared dialogues. In materials for teaching, the structural linguists have helped to develop pattern drills for disks, tapes, and textbooks. Also, they have written manuals of applied linguistics which help teachers to understand better the formation of the language they are teaching and to teach it more effectively. Examples of these helpful manuals are: Robert L. Politzer, *Teaching French: An Introduction to Applied Linguistics* (Boston: Ginn and Company, 1960); Robert L. Politzer and Charles N. Staubach, *Teaching Spanish: A Linguistic Orientation* (Boston: Ginn and Company, 1961). Developments in contrastive linguistics (see Chapter VIII) promise much future help.

In an informative article, "Applied Linguistics in the Classroom," William G. Moulton discusses some of the contributions of linguistics to classroom teaching, as well as some of the latest linguistic terminology: "transformation grammar" and "tagmemics." He also reveals another new linguistic theory which separates the vocabulary of all languages into "function words" and "content words." The function words "are the blood and bone of language; content words are fillers which can fit into particular types of slots." [20]

With this newly expressed theory in regard to vocabulary words, linguistic science may be turning back toward the "indispensable words" which appeared on some of the earlier word-frequency lists.

Evaluation of the audio-lingual techniques. The audio-lingual approach has brought a new joy and satisfaction to students and teachers in secondary schools and colleges. The new techniques give students an early fluency in the oral use of the usual speech patterns of the language, stimulating them to further study. Teachers are pleased because their students at the end of two years of study demonstrate a higher proficiency in oral comprehension and in speaking than do other students in conventional classes.

George Scherer of the University of Colorado at Boulder conducted a four-semester experiment (June, 1960–September, 1962) to test the theory that the reading skill of students trained under the audio-lingual method with use of a language laboratory would surpass that of students trained under the conventional grammar-reading method without such laboratory use. Results of his experiment showed Professor Scherer that German students trained under the conventional method tested better at the end of one semester than those trained under the audio-lingual method; by the end of two semesters, however, the latter had caught up with the former, and clearly surpassed them during the third and fourth semesters.[21]

Scherer's experiment recalls earlier studies made which tested language skills according to mode of study.[22] V. A. C. Henmon's study of 1912 tended to prove that auditory presentation of a modern foreign language was superior to that of other modes.[23] Some thirty years before the Scherer experiment, Mary Olga Peters found that the direct method gave better results in the second semester than did the grammar-translation method; the grammar-translation

[20] William G. Moulton, "Applied Linguistics in the Classroom," *PMLA*, LXXVI, No. 2 (May, 1961), 1–6.

[21] George A. C. Scherer, "The German Teaching Experiment at the University of Colorado." Unpublished thirteen-page report.

[22] For a detailed report, see Charles H. Handschin, *Modern Language Teaching* (New York:Harcourt, Brace & World, Inc., 1940), pp. 70–75.

[23] V. A. C. Henmon, "The Relation between Mode of Presentation and Retention," *Psychological Review*, XIX (March, 1912), 79–96.

method, however, yielded higher test results in the first semester.[24] In the last decade of the nineteenth century Professor H. Münsterberg discovered that study aloud produced better results than silent study.[25] Perhaps the Münsterberg study forecast the long-range benefits from the use of the language laboratory: that the repetition of drill exercises in the laboratory (the studying aloud) would help the students to learn language skills better.

A recent study completed by Raymond F. Keating, Research Fellow of the Institute of Administrative Research at Teachers College, Columbia University, showed that the language laboratory was of negative value to secondary school students. About 5,000 students of French in 21 school districts, all from schools which belong to the Metropolitan School Study Council, New York, were studied. Those students who did not use the language laboratory scored higher on tests than those who did in the areas of reading comprehension, listening comprehension, and speech production. In the last-mentioned area, after one year of instruction the use of the language laboratory seemed to give the students an advantage.[26]

Reaction to the audio-lingual approach. Adverse reactions to some of the extreme points of view of the exponents of the audio-lingual approach soon developed. These centered around the following:

1. *Bilingualism.* Claims that the audio-lingual method would produce bilingual students in a short period of time did not materialize; and many teachers became disillusioned as they realized that more time, not less, would be required if the reading and writing skills were to be developed on a par with those of listening and speaking.

2. *Prereading period.* The prereading period, during which the students heard and repeated foreign phrases but never saw them in print, was too long. In some extreme cases books were kept away from the students for a whole semester. Many students learn faster

---

24 Mary Olga Peters, "An Experimental Comparison of Grammar-Translation Method with Direct Method in Teaching French," *Modern Language Journal,* XVIII (May, 1934), 528–42.

25 H. Münsterberg, "Studies from Harvard University Psychological Laboratory, Memory (Audible and Visual Presentation)," *Psychological Review,* I (May, 1894), 34–39.

26 From an article in the "New York Times" of May 14, 1963.

through the eye than through the ear, and these were held back by the long audio-lingual period.

3. *Use of English.* The student's mother tongue was to be eliminated, but teachers found that such an extreme practice was not desirable. English was needed at times to clarify vocabulary items and to explain certain grammatical structures.

4. *Teaching of grammar.* Grammar was not to be taught to the students until a much later period, after the structures had been "overlearned." The brighter students, however, became curious about the structural drills which they were repeating, and wanted explanations. Many teachers began to teach grammar again as a short cut to faster comprehension.

5. *Concept of culture.* Culture was presented as "everyday living" rather than *belles-lettres* or fine arts. The reading of newspapers and magazines did not present the genius of a people as well as did its masterpieces of art, music, and literature, and teachers became critical of the omissions.

6. *Repetitive drills.* Memorization of drills became a monotonous procedure in many classes, unless the teachers varied them and made them interesting. Moreover, the constant participation of the teacher in these pattern drills through supplying basic and supplementary materials placed a greater strain on him than ever before.

Criticisms of aspects of the audio-lingual approach will result, no doubt, in modifications of its methodology. However, the basic theory behind its arrangement of the language skills in the "natural" order of listening, speaking, reading, and writing seems good; and the stimulus the new approach has given to the creation of new teaching materials based on linguistic science is a significant advance in the teaching of modern foreign languages in the United States.

Textbooks for Modern Foreign Languages

Early textbooks. Methods of teaching modern foreign languages were clearly reflected by the early textbooks used in American schools. Since Latin was the principal language taught in secondary schools from colonial days until the 1940's, and Latin and Greek were preferred in colleges until almost the close of the nineteenth century, textbooks used for teaching the classical languages served as models for the preparation of modern foreign language texts. In the early colonial days, most of these texts had to be brought from abroad. Some which were originally printed in England were later printed in the colonies.

The early grammars for French and German were similar to the Latin-grammar texts in format, with formal presentation of grammar. In each lesson they gave the rules to be observed, gave a list of vocabulary items, including idioms and proverbs to be learned, presented some illustrative sentences in the foreign language, and gave sentences in English which were to be turned back into the foreign language by the students. Many of these sentences functioned as moral precepts in addition to carrying the burden of language instruction.

Many of the early readers were texts which accompanied certain grammars, some with ingenious interlinear coding devices which gave the students aids on word order, idioms, tenses, and cases. The purpose of such readers was to help the student translate accurately into English, using a good style. It should come as no surprise that students "read" very few pages each semester.

Twentieth-century textbooks. Modern foreign language textbooks in the twentieth century are numerous, reflecting each of the major teaching methods in vogue. (Within the compass of this book, it would be impossible to list the names of all the writers of successful language texts and the titles of their books. The titles herein listed serve only as objective illustrations of certain approaches to language learning.)

The big change from the grammar method to the reading method in the 1930's produced recognition grammars, graded reading texts, word-frequency lists, idiom lists, and various types of language tests. Helen Eddy and Grace Cochran of the State University of Iowa conducted experiments among high school students using the "Chicago French Series," and later wrote or edited several texts which featured the reading aim. These were labeled the "Eddy Series," and were published by the University of Chicago Press. Evaluation of the "Eddy Series" was carried out by using the following American Council Tests: Henmon Vocabulary Test, Cheydleur Grammar Test, and Coleman Silent Reading Test.

Because Algernon Coleman, secretary of the Committee on Modern Language Teaching, was a professor at the University of

Chicago, this institution became a center for the development of books featuring the "reading method." Otto Bond wrote many texts; his *Graded French Readers* were widely used. Peter Hagboldt developed a series of *Graded German Readers,* and Carlos Castillo (with Colley Sparkman), produced a series of *Graded Spanish Readers.* D. C. Heath and Company published these French, German, and Spanish graded readers. Several other companies produced graded language series, American Book Company, Houghton Mifflin, and Oxford University Press being among the most prolific.

The Army developed its own language teaching materials based on texts prepared by structural linguists, as did the Foreign Service Institute at a later date. The Army's use of pattern drill to teach language structure was revived in the audio-lingual approach, as pointed out in this chapter.

The Audio-Lingual Materials, known also as the Glastonbury Materials, were the chief examples of the audio-lingual approach (see Chapter V). The Audio-Lingual Materials featured dialogues, pattern drills, and cultural readings for French, German, Italian, Russian, and Spanish. Four levels of instructional materials were being prepared, covering six years of study (grades 7–12).

The Modern Language Association's textbook, *Modern Spanish* (New York: Harcourt, Brace, & World, Inc., 1960), was the first audio-lingual textbook for college use. It started a swing to audio-lingual texts, with emphasis on applied linguistics, as the following titles illustrate: *Basic Conversational French* (1962); *Basic Conversational Italian* (1963); *Learning French the Modern Way,* Book I (1963); *German One: For Laboratory and Classroom* (1962); *Spoken Russian* (1963); *Learning Spanish the Modern Way,* Book I (1963); *Español: Hablar y Leer* (1962); and *A Structural Course in Spanish* (1963).

By 1963, major publishers of beginning textbooks in modern foreign languages were featuring texts written in the new key and published after 1960. A few more-or-less traditional grammars, however, still enjoyed widescale use. These carried in their titles an indication of their approach, using such phrases as "concept approach," "cultural approach," "essentials of," and "foundation course." Accompanying many of these were disks or tapes on which were recorded the foreign language "reading materials": dialogues, pattern drills, and essays on culture. Reading of literature written in the foreign language was usually done on intermediate and advanced levels.

With the emphasis on self-help for students through mechanical and other devices, the beginning language textbook of the future may be constructed on the "teaching-machine" principle, with habit-forming drills presented, followed by exercises of application on the same page, but with answers ("reinforcement") given immediately on another page. Such books could help to eliminate much of the teacher's drudgery in connection with correcting students' homework, and would give the student correct language to use immediately.

Testing

Grammar tests. From approximately 1875, when Harvard began to require French or German for admission, until around 1930, when the Modern Language Study developed new types of examinations, grammar tests were used almost exclusively as measures of a student's ability and achievement in foreign languages. These were the traditional grammar-translation tests consisting of a paragraph in the foreign language to be translated into English, grammar questions requiring conjugation of verbs or declension of nouns, and English sentences of a wide assortment to be written in the foreign language. In 1899 the Committee of Twelve put into its report specimen grammar-question papers for three different levels. The College Entrance Examination Board and many colleges began to use this type of examination around 1900, making few changes until 1911. After this date, changes gradually occurred, such as completion questions on grammar, questions on pronunciation and culture, and free compositions. These questions were fairly easy to formulate, were precise in information called for, and were easy to evaluate in an objective manner. Test scores were used as prognostic (to predict a high school student's success in college language courses), and as achievement (measuring his past success as a language student).

Standardized written tests. Under the discussion of the reading method earlier in this chapter, reference was made to the tests developed under the Modern Foreign Language Study by Algernon Coleman, V. A. C. Henmon and others, and Ben D. Wood. Wood tested approximately 50,000 students by using objective-type tests, and he found the tests to be reliable measurements of the students' progress in certain language skills. Three series of standardized tests for French, German, and Spanish resulted from his experiments: (1) American Council, (2) Columbia Research Bureau, and (3) Coöperative Test Service.

The American Council had tests to examine vocabulary, grammar, silent reading, composition, and aural comprehension; the Columbia Research Bureau tests covered vocabulary, comprehension, and grammar; and the Coöperative Test Service tests were for reading, vocabulary, and grammar. National norms applicable to college and secondary school students were developed from the use of these tests. Many other standardized tests were developed in subsequent years.[27] Teachers considered these tests as good indicators of the mechanical aspects of language learning, but they did not measure the student's creative ability or his oral competency.

Oral tests. Aural-oral tests were slow in making an appearance. They were difficult to produce for general use because of three major problems which they presented: (1) the technical construction of the tests (which items to include and how to present them); (2) how to examine the student over items presented (by pencil and paper, by oral response, or by both means); and (3) the matter of achieving widespread distribution of such tests. With the invention of the electronic tape recorder and magnetic tape, the third problem was partially solved; tapes could be sent to centers where students were tested. The second problem remained the most vexing, because the tests usually measured listening comprehension (aural ability) rather than proficiency in speaking (oral ability). Where tape recorders were available for student use in classrooms or in language laboratories, students could record vocal responses to oral stimuli given them.

The MLA Cooperative Language Tests, prepared for secondary school students of French, German, Italian, Russian, and Spanish, did examine the student's speaking skill in addition to the skills of listening comprehension, reading, and writing. The "MLA Proficiency Tests for Teachers and Advanced Students" likewise tested the college student's oral ability by having him record responses on tape (see Chapter V). Tests of the College Entrance Examination Board also included listening comprehension after 1960.

---

[27] See Charles H. Handschin, *Modern Language Teaching* (New York: Harcourt, Brace & World, Inc., 1940), pp. 120–21.

CHAPTER IV

Foreign Languages in
the Elementary Schools

Early in the twentieth century many well-to-do families employed governesses to teach young children foreign languages in
the home. A few influential families were able to have school
boards include the teaching of foreign languages in the elementary
grades in private academies and in public schools. German study in
the grades had become entrenched in the public schools in the nineteenth century and had carried over into the twentieth. Many
schools, however, had to abandon such teaching because of the ex-
penses involved. As early as 1903, Chicago had dropped German
from the first four grades, and Cleveland had done likewise in 1907;
but in 1910, 13 principal United States cities offered German in
the elementary schools, some with large enrollments. In 1914,
Cincinnati had a total public elementary school enrollment of
43,291, and 14,649 (33.8 per cent) were enrolled in German. In
1917–18, the German enrollment had dropped to about 7,000,
and it disappeared from the Cincinnati schools when such instruction was made illegal in World War I. Buffalo, New York, and
New York City also had large German enrollments.[1]

French was not strongly established in public elementary schools
of the United States in the early part of the twentieth century, being
offered chiefly in a few city schools in the East. In 1909, the Committee on College Entrance Requirements, appointed by the New
England Modern Language Association, reported that only three
schools taught French in the grades, where it formed part of a six-
year high school sequence.[2] The "Cleveland Plan," begun in 1921
to teach French to superior children, is the oldest of the current
elementary school programs.

Polish and Italian were taught in a few large public elementary

---

[1] E. W. Bagster-Collins, *Studies in Modern Language Teaching*, pp. 16–23.
[2] Bagster-Collins, *op. cit.*, p. 24.

schools through 1917. Spanish received its impetus from the Good Neighbor Policy of the 1940's, the chief elementary school enrollments being in Arizona, California, Florida, New Mexico, and Texas.

After 1952. Foreign languages in the elementary schools (FLES) grew into a nationwide educational phenomenon in the United States after May 2, 1952. On that date, Earl J. McGrath, then United States Commissioner of Education, told a teachers meeting in Saint Louis that the events of World War II had convinced him that foreign languages were "a very important element in general education." He called upon American educators "from the elementary schools to the top levels of the university system" to give immediate attention to the question of providing foreign language study to as many citizens as possible. Response to Commissioner McGrath's address was immediate and nationwide, cutting across all educational levels.

The National Conference on the Role of Foreign Languages in American Schools, sponsored by the United States Office of Education, was held in Washington, D.C., on January 15 and 16, 1953. Approximately 350 persons, representing a great cross section of American educators and laymen, were invited to the conference. From this conference many of the participants returned to their home communities to start experimental programs in FLES. How fast the movement spread is best told by a few statistics.

From a total of only 145 communities and a pupil enrollment of 145,643, reported by Kenneth Mildenberger in 1953,[3] FLES had spread by 1959 to over 8,000 schools with 1,227,006 pupils enrolled, a 742.5 per cent of increase over 1953. The 1,227,006 pupils in regular and televised FLES programs were enrolled in schools as follows: public elementary, 1,030,097 (84 per cent); independent (private), 35,092 (2.9 per cent); laboratory (on-campus), 12,304 (1 per cent); Catholic elementary, 146,025 (11.9 per cent); and Lutheran elementary, 3,488 (6.2 per cent).[4]

FLES in regular public school programs. In the public ele-

---

[3] Kenneth W. Mildenberger, *Status of Foreign Language Study in American Elementary Schools, Fall Term, 1953* (Washington, D.C.: U.S. Office of Education, March, 1954).

[4] Marjorie Breunig, "Foreign Languages in the Elementary Schools of the United States, 1959–60," in *Reports of Surveys and Studies in the Teaching of Modern Foreign Languages* (New York: Modern Language Association, 1961), pp. 1–3.

mentary schools of the United States in 1959–60 (excluding the televised and non-public school programs), 1217 communities reported a total of 692,716 pupils enrolled in foreign languages from the kindergarten through grade eight. Enrollments and per cents for six of the languages taught were as follows:

Language	Enrollment K–8	Per Cent of Total (692,716)
Spanish	485,825	70.1
French	184,651	26.7
German	17,535	2.5
Russian	1,384	0.2
Italian	1,188	0.2
Latin	844	0.1
All others	1,289	0.2

Non-public school programs. In the regular (nontelevised) programs offered in the non-public elementary schools, French was the principal language, ahead of Spanish in all types of schools except the Lutheran, where German had 58.6 per cent of the totals. It must be kept in mind, however, that the enrollments in non-public school FLES programs were small in comparison with those in public schools. A comparison between French and Spanish in the non-public schools follows.

Type of School	Total FLES Enrollment K–8	French, Enroll- ment	K–8 Per Cent	Spanish, Enroll- ment	K–8 Per Cent
Catholic	146,025	101,155	69.3	24,234	16.6
Independent (private)	32,208	25,139	73.4	5,186	15.2
Laboratory (on-campus)	11,782	5,811	49.3	4,854	41.2
Lutheran	3,488	484	13.9	858	24.6
Total U.S.A.	193,503	132,589	68.6	35,132	18.2

Televised FLES programs. Many public and non-public elementary schools offered televised instruction in foreign languages in 1959, with Spanish and French the usual languages. Public schools reported a total of 337,381 television pupils: Spanish, 232,810 (69 per cent); French, 101,421 (30.1 per cent); others, 3,150 (.9 per cent). Of the non-public schools, nine independent elementary schools reported a total of 884 pupils, all taking French; and seven laboratory (on-campus) schools had 522 television pupils: French, 115 (22.1 per cent); and Spanish, 407 (77.9 per cent).

One of the widely used television French courses was "Parlons Français," organized in 1959 in Boston by the Modern Language Project of the Massachusetts Council for Public Schools. The course consisted of 60 lessons, each of 15 minutes duration. It was put on film for use in the classroom, and on videotapes for educational and commercial open- and closed-circuit television stations. Two lessons were given each week, and there were teacher-preparation programs for each lesson. The course was offered to pupils in the third, fourth, and fifth grades. The teacher of "Parlons Français" was Madame Anne Slack, a native Frenchwoman who had previously taught televised French lessons with outstanding success in the elementary schools of Schenectady, New York.

FLES in city school systems. From 1953 through 1959, the FLES movement spread from a total of 684 schools in 33 states and the District of Columbia to over 8,000 schools, all states and the District of Columbia being represented. Most of these programs in the grades were located at first in small communities where local people taught on a voluntary basis. In several city school systems, however, twentieth-century FLES programs had been established or restored before 1950: Cleveland (1921), Oakwood-Dayton (1924), Niagara Falls (1930), New York City (1934–36), Detroit (1935), Los Angeles (1943), and San Diego (1944), to name only a few.

New York City, by official action of its School Board, in 1958 introduced French and Spanish as part of an enrichment program for intellectually gifted children.[5] In 1962, French, Italian, and Spanish were offered to "gifted children" in grades four, five, and six, with over 7,000 pupils enrolled.

Some additional city school systems which had extensive FLES programs in the 1960's were Washington, D.C.; Houston, Texas; Saint Louis, Missouri; Chicago, Illinois; Fairfield, Connecticut; and Springfield, Massachusetts.

Problems with success. The rapid rise of foreign languages in the elementary schools brought accompanying problems:

1. *Teacher shortage.* Many schools found it impossible to staff

---

[5] Theodore Huebener, *How to Teach Foreign Languages Effectively* (New York: New York University Press, 1959), p. 167.

the FLES programs with qualified language teachers, and regular elementary classroom teachers, with little or no foreign language training, were pressed into service. By using televised language lessons, and by taking in-service training, many of these teachers achieved creditable results. Other schools engaged high school or college language teachers to come two or more times each week to teach languages in the grades. In some communities foreign-born persons were the teachers.

2. *Battle of the budget.* Coupled with finding capable FLES teachers was the problem of adding enough money to the school budget to pay them, and then getting the added sum approved by the voters. In some communities there were repeated battles of the ballots, with FLES programs being voted in or out according to the mood of the taxpayers who attended the meetings.

3. *For whom?* A school had to decide whether or not to offer foreign languages to all its pupils in certain grades, or only to the most gifted. If all children were together in a language program, at what stage should the very weak pupils be eliminated? Most of the programs included all the children in a school grade, and the less able were dropped at the end of grade six.

4. *Teaching interval.* Since young children have a short attention span, FLES classes in grades K-2 usually lasted 15 or 20 minutes, and were offered from two to five times per week. In grades 3–6 the teaching period often was from 20 to 30 minutes, three to five times weekly; and in grades 7 and 8 the class period was usually 40–45 minutes, three times a week.

5. *Choice of language.* Some schools arbitrarily chose a language for which they had elementary school teachers who could teach it, or because the high school language teacher offered to help; others sent ballots to the parents and asked them to choose the language; still other schools started all beginning children in French one year and all in Spanish the next.

6. *Continuity of study.* Schools which offered foreign languages in the senior, but not in the junior, high school had to decide whether or not to start a FLES program which might be discontinued for an interval of one to three years. In other schools which had continuous language programs, there was the problem of how to organize language classes for pupils who had come up through the FLES program. If pupils continued through junior into senior

high school, the senior high school language program had to be organized to accommodate (a) those who started in FLES, and (b) those who had never had any previous experience with the language. In many schools, tests for proficiency, given at the end of each semester, determined in which program a student stayed.

Many schools did offer foreign language programs in the lower grades and then discontinued them at the end of grade 6. Other schools required the less able pupils to drop language work at the end of the sixth grade. Junior high school language classes were more formal and demanding, usually requiring reading and writing in addition to the oral work. The basic Course I often started in grade 8 for those who had had three or four years of FLES, thus permitting a secondary school pupil to take five years of language, the last of which might be for advanced placement with or without credit in college.

7. *Teaching materials.* For a few years after 1953, there were very few syllabi, guides, and other materials to help the FLES teachers. In 1955 the Modern Language Association published *Beginning French in Grade 3,* followed later by its *Continuing French in Grade 4,* and by two similar guides for German. Guides prepared for Spanish started with grade 3 and continued through grade 6.[6]

MLA policy statement on FLES.[7] In January, 1961, the Modern Language Association issued its revised policy statement on FLES; the first had appeared in 1956. The concluding section of the revised statement summarized the basic problems confronting foreign language teaching in the elementary schools.

> H. *Cautions.* A FLES program should be instituted only if: (1) it is an integral and serious part of the school day; (2) it is an integral and serious part of the total foreign-language program in the school system; (3) there is close articulation with later foreign-language learning; (4) there are available FL specialists or elementary-school teachers with an adequate command of the foreign language; (5) there is a planned syllabus and a sequence of appropriate teaching materials; (6) the program has the support of the administration; (7) the high school teachers of the foreign language in the local school system recognize the same long-range

[6] See the *MLA Selective List of Materials,* ed. Mary J. Ollmann (New York: Modern Language Association, 1962), pp. 26, 42, 90.
[7] *PMLA,* LXXVI, No. 2 (May, 1961), vi–vii.

objectives and practice some of the same teaching techniques as the
FLES teachers.

The Modern Language Association held several conferences in
New York City to which specialists in elementary education were
invited to meet with language specialists in order to provide "informed answers" to the questions usually asked concerning foreign
language teaching in the elementary grades. The second conference (June 11–12, 1954) gave detailed answers to 16 questions
based on "Considerations for Initiating a Program of Modern Foreign Languages in an Elementary School." These questions and
answers were given wide dissemination by the Foreign Language
Program of the MLA under the title, "Foreign Languages in Elementary Schools: Some Questions and Answers."

Two basic questions—with answers

1. *Why begin foreign languages in the elementary schools?* Commissioner of Education Earl McGrath answered this question at
the Washington conference on January 15, 1953, giving one "practical" reason and one scientific:

> The proposal then that instruction in modern foreign languages
> be offered in the lower grades of the elementary school rests on
> two propositions. First, more Americans should be able to use a
> foreign language. The best place to reach large numbers of our
> future citizens is in the elementary schools; and second, languages
> should be begun in the early grades because children learn then
> most easily and most precisely.[8]

Commissioner McGrath's scientific reason was given support
less than a month later by Wilder G. Penfield, brain surgeon and
Director of the Montreal Neurological Institute, who said in an
address before the American Academy of Arts and Sciences on
February 11, 1953:

> . . . My plea is that we should let children hear secondary lan-
> guages, properly spoken, at an early age. . . . The duration of
> man's childhood is very long as compared with that of other ani-
> mals, and the early years are normally devoted to learning a lan-
> guage as a means of learning about life. The human brain has a
> plasticity at that time and a specialized capacity for acquiring speech

---

[8] Earl J. McGrath, "Foreign Language Instruction in American Schools," in a
special bulletin issued by D. C. Heath & Company, Boston, 1953, pp. 8–9.

which is lost later. . . . "To everything there is a season and a time to every purpose under heaven." Educators, before all others, must realize that this is particularly true of the "organ of the mind." Physiological evolution causes it to specialize in the learning of language before the ages of 10 to 14. After that gradually, inevitably, it seems to become rigid, slow, less receptive.[9]

In addition to the practical and scientific reasons given for starting a foreign language early in the grades, another more philosophical reason could be given: A foreign language gives the young child a better preparation for understanding the big world he lives in; it gives a third dimension, "my world," to those of "my family" and "my country." By immersing himself in the language and customs of a foreign people, a child begins unconsciously to identify himself with humanity in general.

2. *Should a FLES program be started if unbroken continuity into secondary school cannot be assured?* The MLA Policy Statement clearly states the desired goal: "We must sharpen our definition of FLES. It is not an end in itself but the elementary-school (K–6) part of a language learning program that should extend unbroken through grade 12." [10]

There is no quarrel with this desideratum; the rigid application of this policy to specific school situations, however, would be too restrictive, in this writer's opinion, for the following reasons:

1. The status-quo languages in the secondary schools would always determine the languages started in the grades and might discourage the extension of other languages into a school system. For example, Spanish and French (in that order) are the chief modern languages offered in secondary school and in FLES programs. An elementary school may have on its faculty a certified teacher of German birth who teaches sciences and who would like to organize and teach German in the grades as well. By allowing the German to teach his native language in the grades, an interest in extending German into the secondary school might result, and German might already be established in the high school curriculum by the time the FLES students got there. The same argument could be applied to any of the non-status-quo languages.

---

[9] Wilder G. Penfield, "A Consideration of the Neurophysiological Mechanisms of Speech and Some Educational Consequences," in *Proceedings of the American Academy of Arts and Sciences,* LXXXII, No. 5 (April, 1953), 212–13.

[10] *PMLA,* LXXVI, No. 2 (May, 1961), vi, "B. Redefinition."

2. In the status-quo languages, often there is no junior high school foreign language program; yet it exists in senior high. If a child took French or Spanish from grade 3 through 6, he would acquire valuable ear training, and his oral fluency would not be entirely lost during the hiatus of two years in his language program. He would have a better start on formal language study in high school for having had some earlier language experience in the grades.

3. Approximately forty per cent of American high schools offered no modern foreign languages in 1960. If language programs should not be started in elementary schools in these communities until programs first existed in the secondary schools, the whole process of starting languages eventually in high school might be unduly delayed.

4. There are some unmeasurable residual values of appreciation and understanding which a child receives from any foreign language skillfully and sympathetically taught over a period of three or four years. Like music in the grades, a foreign language offers a pupil an opportunity for self-expression, enjoyment, and appreciation.

Impact of FLES. When parents, teachers, school administrators, and professional educators saw the ease with which young children adapted to a foreign language through the oral method, an era of good will was ushered in for foreign languages in general. High school and college teachers saw demonstrations of the audio-lingual techniques in action, and many of them revitalized their teaching accordingly. FLES was the link between the Army method and the audio-lingual, and served to spark a new era in the preparation of modern foreign language teachers and in the designing of language textbooks and other materials for all academic levels. The success of foreign languages in the elementary schools touched off a renewed interest in language learning and child development on the part of language teachers, neurologists, psychiatrists, psychologists, and sociologists. Elementary, high school, and college language teachers began to discuss common problems and to work out effective teaching techniques. Interdisciplinary cooperation between specialists in education and specialists in foreign languages grew as the two groups beat their academic swords into plowshares and tilled the fertile field of language learning. Truly, a little child had led them.

CHAPTER V

The National Defense Education Act of 1958

On September 2, 1958, President Dwight D. Eisenhower signed into law the National Defense Education Act of 1958. Congress originally authorized the Act for the period September, 1958, to June, 1962, but in 1961 extended the time until June, 1964. The need for the Act had been established early in 1957 by testimony given before committees of the United States Office of Education, House of Representatives, and Senate. The passage of the Act dramatized the urgent national need for more competent students of science, mathematics, and modern foreign languages in the educational system of the United States; it signaled a turning back to an emphasis on these academic subjects which had been neglected during the popularity of the core curriculum, vocational, and life-adjustment programs. The purpose of the Act was stated in Title I, General Provisions, Section 101.

> The Congress hereby finds and declares that the security of the Nation requires the fullest development of the mental resources and technical skills of its young men and women. The present emergency demands that additional and more adequate educational opportunities be made available. The defense of this Nation depends upon the mastery of modern techniques developed from complex scientific principles. It depends as well upon the discovery and development of new principles, new techniques, and new knowledge.
>
> We must increase our efforts to identify and educate more of the talent of our Nation. This requires programs that will give assurance that no student of ability will be denied an opportunity for higher education because of financial need; will correct as rapidly as possible the existing imbalances in our educational programs which have led to an insufficient proportion of our population educated in science, mathematics, and modern foreign languages and trained in technology.

The Congress reaffirms the principle and declares that the States and local communities have and must retain control over and primary responsibility for public education. The national interest requires, however, that the Federal Government give assistance to education for programs which are important to our defense.

To meet the present educational emergency requires additional effort at all levels of government. It is therefore the purpose of this Act to provide substantial assistance in various forms to individuals, and to States and their subdivisions, in order to insure trained manpower of sufficient quality and quantity to meet the national defense needs of the United States.[1]

Status of foreign languages, 1958. There had certainly been neglect in modern foreign language study. A survey of 1958 offerings and enrollments in foreign languages, conducted by the Modern Language Association for the U.S. Office of Education, revealed the following facts: (1) Only half of the secondary schools in the United States offered at least one modern language; (2) only one out of every seven students enrolled in a language when it was offered; (3) one out of four students continued beyond the second year of study; and (4) a total of 9,429 students were enrolled in only five of the 24 languages which the Commissioner of Education had classified as "critical" to the National needs: Chinese, 21; Hebrew, 4,255; Polish, 499; Portuguese, 599; and Russian, 4,055.[2] The colleges and universities had reported a total of only 8,013 students in 60 "unusual" languages in the fall of 1958 (see Chapter II). After 1958, however, enrollments in modern foreign languages increased rapidly because certain parts (titles) of the National Defense Education Act were designed to support more and better modern language teaching.

Title II: loans to students. For the fiscal years 1959–62, Congress appropriated $202,000,000 for loans to full-time college students. A student could borrow up to $1,000 per year for five years, if he was fully qualified. Repayments started a year after graduation and were spread over ten equal, annual payments. If a student should teach in a public elementary or secondary school for five years, half of his loan would be canceled.

Title III: financial assistance for strengthening science, mathe-

---

[1] Public Law 85–864, 85th Congress, H. R. 13247, pp. 2–3.
[2] J. Wesley Childers, "Foreign Language Offerings and Enrollments in Public Secondary Schools, Fall 1958," in *PMLA,* LXXVI, No. 2B (May, 1961), 36–50.

matics, and modern foreign language instruction. Inadequate teaching of modern foreign languages was one of the reasons for their steady decline. Title III gave money to the states and territories to help them strengthen language teaching in the public elementary and secondary schools. Each state had to submit and direct its own plan for improving instruction, matching dollar for dollar the amount received from the federal government. Congress authorized a total of $70,000,000 each year for equipment and materials and minor remodeling, and $5,000,000 a year for supervisory and related services. The full amount was not appropriated, however, because of the inability of many states to match the federal funds. Private schools could apply directly to the U.S. Office of Education for loans for these purposes. Chief uses of Title III money were the following:

1. *Modern language supervisors.* Many of the language teachers in each state were inadequately prepared for their work and needed supervisory help. Before 1958, only three states had modern language supervisors or consultants; by the end of 1962, 37 states had a total of 57 language specialists on their staffs. These supervisors kept the language teachers informed about new books and materials for teaching languages, organized in-service training courses for teachers, sent out bulletins containing information (including tips on teaching), and personally visited as many of the individual teachers as possible each year. In addition, the supervisors usually coordinated facts and figures on language enrollments within their states, and served as public-relations personnel. Their services greatly aided in improving modern language teaching on all instructional levels.

2. *Language laboratories.* States and territories were quick to respond to federal assistance in regard to the purchase of language laboratories. In 1957, one year prior to the passage of the NDEA, the U.S. Office of Education reported a total of 46 language laboratories in public high schools;[3] in 1960, the same office had compiled "an unofficial file of about 2,500 secondary schools having some

---

[3] Marjorie C. Johnston and Catharine C. Seerley, *Foreign Language Laboratories in Schools and Colleges,* U.S. Department of Health, Education, and Welfare, Bulletin 1959, No. 3 (Washington, D.C.: United States Government Printing Office, 1961), p. 7.

kind of language laboratory"; [4] and at the end of 1962, the estimate was well over 5,000.

During the period 1958–62, more than 180,000 local school projects were approved for the acquisition of equipment for instruction in science, mathematics, and modern foreign languages, or for minor remodeling and repairs to improve instruction in these subjects. Since each state made and administered its own plan and established its own priorities in the approval of projects, there was great variation in the per cents of funds allocated to the three subject fields and to the different levels of instruction. Nationwide, about 75 per cent of the funds were used for science, eight per cent for mathematics, and 17 per cent for modern foreign languages. A total of approximately $57,000,000 was allocated to the purchase of equipment and materials for modern foreign languages from 1958–62.

Title IV: fellowships.   College language teachers were in short supply in 1958 when an estimated 15,000 more were needed. To encourage more students to take graduate work and later teach in colleges and universities, Congress authorized "such sums as may be necessary" to support as many as 5,500 fellowships. Each fellow received a stipend of $2,000 during the first year, $2,200 during the second, and $2,400 during the third—plus $400 annually for each of his dependents. His college, in addition, received a sum which partly offset the costs of offering the program to the fellow. More than $38,000,000 was spent on this program in the first three years.

Title V: guidance counseling and testing.   Part A of Title V allocated funds to states which submitted their plans for testing and counseling, and which identified students "with outstanding aptitudes and ability." Part B allocated money for institutes set up in colleges and universities to train personnel for guidance and counseling. Presumably, strong language students might be discovered and encouraged through this program. To date, under Title III, rather than Title V, one publication has been issued for guidance counselors in the modern foreign language field.[5]

---

[4] Joseph C. Hutchinson, *Modern Foreign Languages in High School: The Language Laboratory*, U.S. Department of Health, Education, and Welfare, OE–27013, Bulletin 1961, No. 23 (Washington, D.C.: United States Government Printing Office, 1961), pp. 3–4.

[5] *Modern Foreign Languages; A Counselor's Guide*, Department of Health, Education, and Welfare, U.S. Office of Education Bulletin 1960, No. 2 (Washington, D.C.: United States Government Printing Office, 1960).

Title VI: language development. Recognizing that a well-trained teacher is the prime need for an effective modern language program, Congress allocated more than $30,500,000 for Title VI for the first two years of its existence; approximately $21,900,000 was appropriated during this interval to carry out teacher training and research provisions of the Title.

Part A of Title VI supported (1) fellowships in the critical languages, (2) language and area centers for these languages, and (3) research and studies concerning language instruction. Between 1959 and 1962, under the category of research, 214 research contracts were awarded at a total cost of $10,381,320.

Language and area centers. Between 1959 and 1963, many language and area centers were established in American colleges and universities to train specialists in certain languages not commonly taught in the United States, but which were needed by government agencies, business, industry, and education. In its first four years of operation, Title VI spent $6,035,660 for such centers, matched by at least an equal amount from the institutions operating them. The 53 area centers established in 1962–63 in 33 colleges and universities were distributed as follows: East Asia, 11; Southeast Asia, 3; South Asia, 6; Near and Middle East, 8; Slavic, 10; Slavic-East Asia, 2; Uralic-Altaic, 2; African, 4, and Latin American, 7.[6]

Critical languages. After specialists of the American Council of Learned Societies reported on a study made of languages needed in the United States, the United States Commissioner of Education listed 24 languages as essential to national defense. The first group included six (Spanish was added later): Arabic, Chinese, Hindi-Urdu, Japanese, Portuguese, and Russian. The second group contained 18: Bengali, Burmese, Finnish, Hebrew (modern), Hungarian, Indonesian-Malay, Khalkha (Outer Mongolia), Korean, Marathi (India), Persian, Polish, Serbo-Croatian, Singhalese (Ceylon), Swahili (East Africa), Tamil (Ceylon and India), Telugu (India), Thai, and Turkish.

A total of 2,389 language fellowships was awarded between 1959 and 1962 to students of these neglected languages, with 1,006 fellowships awarded for the academic year 1962–63. The distribu-

---

[6] United States Department of Health, Education and Welfare, *NDEA and Higher Education,* OE–50024–4 (Washington, D.C.: Office of Education, August, 1962), p. 3.

tion by language of the 2,389 fellowships was as follows: Arabic, 283; Chinese, 332; Hindi-Urdu, 195; Japanese, 289; Portuguese, 177; Russian, 560; Spanish, 100; others, 453.[7]

Research and studies. From 1959 through 1962, 195 language research and study projects, supported by NDEA funds, were authorized by the United States Office of Education. Thirty-four of the 195 were new projects for 1962.[8] In general, these projects for modern foreign languages dealt with teaching materials, proficiency examinations, research into the psychology of language learning, effective teaching methods, national language needs, and the status of language teaching in schools and colleges of the United States. Brief descriptions of some illustrative projects follow.

1. *Teaching materials.* The Glastonbury, Connecticut, Public Schools, under contract with the United States Office of Education, developed basic audio-lingual teaching materials for secondary school (grades 7–12) French, German, Italian, Russian, and Spanish. The first level of these specialized materials was introduced in the fall of 1961; the second, one year later. These Glastonbury materials, produced at the Modern Language Materials Development Center in New York City, were designed for a language-learning sequence of six years.

Materials were developed for the teaching of many neglected languages. Georgetown University produced an English-Arabic dictionary and a grammar for each of the three principal Arabic dialects: Iraqui, Syrian, and Moroccan. Materials, under other contracts, were prepared by different centers for the teaching of Arabic and Chinese in the secondary schools and colleges; additional materials were prepared for college teaching of other neglected languages. A conference of language specialists, called by the United States Office of Education in March, 1961, listed 157 neglected languages as the minimum number in which adequate teaching materials should be prepared. For each of these 157 languages there would be a textbook, accompanying recordings, a

---

[7] For detailed listing of American universities and colleges in which these languages are taught, see the MLA's *Report of Surveys and Studies in the Teaching of Modern Foreign Languages,* Chapters V, VI, and VIII. See also the report by Austin E. Fife and Marion L. Nielsen, "Conference on Neglected Languages," Chapter XI of the above publication.

[8] United States Department of Health, Education, and Welfare, *National Defense Language Development Research and Studies, Fiscal 1962,* OE–12014–62 (Washington, D.C.: U.S. Government Printing Office, 1962), p. 1.

reader, a reference grammar, and a dictionary. For the 157 languages, 628 volumes would be required; at present, 140 volumes have been started.

Lists of teaching materials were compiled by the Modern Language Association for language teachers in the elementary and secondary schools. The first list, *Materials List for Use by Teachers of Modern Languages,* edited by Douglas Alden and supported by NDEA Title VII funds, appeared in 1959. The second, a revised and enlarged list, was published in 1962. The new list contained 1,850 items relating to ten languages: French, German, Italian, Modern Hebrew, Norwegian, Polish, Portuguese, Russian, Spanish, and Swedish.[9] Master teachers from all sections of the United States were asked to evaluate books, films, filmstrips, pictures, records, slides, and tapes, and to give an evaluation which would point out the strength or weakness of the items and would show the teacher in what way he might be able to use them.

2. *Proficiency tests.* The "MLA Proficiency Tests for Teachers and Advanced Students" were developed for French, German, Italian, Russian, and Spanish. These tests, directed by Wilmarth H. Starr and compiled by approximately 100 language teachers in cooperation with the Educational Testing Service of Princeton, New Jersey, showed the examinee's competency in seven areas of language preparation: listening comprehension, speaking, reading, writing, linguistic analysis, culture, and professional preparation. These tests were especially applicable to graduates of teacher-preparatory programs in modern foreign languages, and scores on the seven separate areas of competence indicated the degree of proficiency of the teacher candidate in each area. State certifying agencies could now use scores from these proficiency tests as a final basis for certifying modern language teachers, rather than the common, unsatisfactory practice of requiring only a certain number of semester hours of study.

For high schools, the MLA Cooperative Foreign Language Tests were prepared to test listening comprehension, speaking, reading, and writing for French, German, Italian, Russian, and Spanish. These tests, under the direction of Nelson Brooks, were prepared in

[9] MLA, ed. Mary J. Ollmann, *Selective List of Materials for Use by Teachers of Modern Foreign Languages in Elementary and Secondary Schools* (New York: Modern Language Association, 1962).

cooperation with the Educational Testing Service and consisted of two levels: (1) a "lower test" for pupils who started in grade 9 and who had progressed halfway through grade 10; and (2) an "upper test" for pupils when they were halfway through grade 12.

3. *Language learning.* Learning theory as applied to modern foreign languages has been supported by the U.S. Office of Education in 27 contracts since 1959. In the Somerville, New Jersey public schools, pupils studied either Spanish or French from the third to the eighth grade in an experiment designed to determine whether the achievement of these students in other subjects was lessened because of the time devoted to foreign language study. The research indicated that achievement in other subjects had not been lessened, and that the students were one year ahead of those who began language study in the ninth grade. Consequently, the pupils who had started language study in the elementary grades were able to take advanced placement examinations.

The University of California at Los Angeles completed a one-year study of factors which lead to achievement in modern foreign languages. A special part of this study concerned the under-achiever in junior high school foreign language classes. The research was continued in 1962 at Ohio State University.

Research in the use of programmed-instruction materials has been subsidized by NDEA funds. The University of Michigan developed programs for self-instruction in hearing, speaking, reading, and writing Chinese, Russian, Thai, Spanish, and French. (Chapter VI of this monograph relates more about the Michigan experiment.) Such programming in modern foreign languages promised to be useful for training personnel for foreign service, as well as being useful for the independent learner in schools and colleges.

4. *Studies and surveys.* From 1959–61 the Modern Language Association, under contract with the U.S. Office of Education, conducted a series of 28 studies and surveys on the status of foreign language teaching at all instructional levels in the United States. Over a period of two years, as these investigations were completed, they were submitted to the United States Office of Education for subsequent dissemination to the public. Twenty-one of the studies were published in a large volume of 326 triple-columned pages; [10]

---

10 Modern Language Association, *Reports of Surveys and Studies in the Teaching of Modern Foreign Languages* (New York: Modern Language Association, 1961).

the other seven were published separately.[11] These studies included reports of many aspects of language teaching and learning in the United States: data on foreign language enrollments in public elementary and secondary schools, in independent secondary schools, in junior and senior colleges, and in universities; data on degrees, language majors, language-teaching practices, and language faculties in colleges and universities; information on teacher-education curriculums in the modern foreign languages; and recommendations and work-papers from various conferences.

Special studies included were: language schools not under academic auspices; language teaching by television; practices in teaching foreign languages in the elementary schools; good teaching practices in high schools; language needs of municipal employees; selective and annotated bibliographies for six cultures (French, German, Hispanic, Italian, Luso-Brazilian, Russian); interrelation between first and second language learning; a study of the academic preparation of language teachers in Connecticut; and histories of the teaching of German and Spanish in the United States.

An annotated international bibliography of research on language teaching (1945–61) received Title VI funds. This work identified contemporary studies and presented needs for further research in the improvement of language teaching. It included a worldwide list of selected research reports completed or in progress since 1945.[12]

Language institutes. Part B of Title VI provided for language institutes where elementary and secondary public and private school teachers or supervisors could receive advanced training, particularly in the use of new teaching methods and new instructional materials. A total of 197 institutes was operated in the summers of 1959–62 (and 21 academic-year institutes), in which more than 10,000 teachers of modern foreign languages received training in the newest techniques of language teaching. The summer institutes grew as

---

[11] Four were statistical surveys of secondary schools (1958–60) and colleges (junior and senior, 1961), previously reported in Chapter II. The additional three were: Anna Balakian, "Certification Requirements for Modern Foreign Language Teachers in American Public Schools (1959–60)," *PMLA,* LXXVI, No. 2 (May, 1961), 20–35; Leonard Cohan and Kenneth Craven, *Science Information Personnel* (New York: Modern Language Association, 1961); and Jeanine Parisier Plottel, "Foreign Language Entrance and Degree Requirements for the B.A. Degree in Accredited Colleges and Universities," *PMLA,* LXXV, No. 4, Part 2 (September, 1960), 14–28.

[12] Howard Lee Nostrand, *et al., Research on Language Teaching: An Annotated International Bibliography for 1945–61* (Seattle, Wash.: University of Washington Press, 1962).

follows: 1959 (12), 1960 (37), 1961 (68), and 1962 (80). Eight of the 80 summer institutes in 1962 were held in foreign countries. The institutes stressed pattern drills, use of language laboratories, study of applied linguistics, integration of language and area study, use of the new MLA proficiency tests, use of new instructional materials, conversation, and composition.

A composite table of summer and academic-year institutes (as of April, 1963) shows the total number of participants and total number of institutes (summer and academic-year) from 1959 through the 1963 projected data. It shows the number of teachers

TABLE 5

LANGUAGE INSTITUTE PROGRAM 1959–63

	Total	1959	1960	1961	1962	1963
Total Number of Participants	15,721	1,002	2,110	3,756	4,413	4,440
Summer	15,155	920	2,003	3,595	4,294	4,343
Acad. Year	566	82	107	161	119	97
Elementary	2,281	84	277	495	527	898
Secondary	13,440	918	1,833	3,261	3,886	3,542
Public	–	958	1,981	3,449	4,060	–
Private	–	44	129	307	353	–
I—level	13,876	1,002	1,940	3,506	3,872	3,556
II—level	1,728	–	170	250	541	767
III—level	57	–	–	–	–	57
II field	60	–	–	–	–	60
Chinese	93	–	–	9	44	40
French	6,431	405	885	1,587	1,786	1,768
German	1,853	140	312	347	590	464
Hebrew	77	–	–	37	–	40
Italian	93	–	28	41	24	–
Japanese	20	–	–	20	–	–
Russian	834	58	89	213	256	218
Spanish	6,320	399	796	1,502	1,713	1,910
No. of FLES programs	102	6	13	25	23	35
No. of FLSS programs	403	31	61	109	109	93
No. of sponsoring institutions	115	16	42 (10)*	71 (41)	81 (58)	79 (64)
No. of institutes	301	16	42	75	85	83

* Numbers in parentheses represent numbers of repeat institutions.

from public and private elementary and secondary schools, the level of the institute, the enrollment by languages, the number of programs for foreign languages in the elementary schools (FLES) and for secondary schools (FLSS), the number of sponsoring institutions, and the total (composite) number of institutes.

Title VII: communications media. In the interval 1958–61, $1,117,370 had been spent under Title VII for 17 modern foreign language research projects. These studies included language teaching by television, audio-visual materials, and instructional films.

Effects of the NDEA on modern foreign languages. The National Defense Education Act of 1958 stimulated the public interest in the study of modern foreign languages much in the same way that the Army method had done 15 years earlier. Editors of newspapers and magazines, as well as publishers of textbooks, were interested in the statistical surveys and research projects. Increased numbers of school boards and school administrators in every state became interested in having effective, meaningful language programs in their schools. More schools afforded pupils the opportunities for language study, and the pupils' response was positive. Language teachers in elementary and secondary schools and in colleges cooperated with state supervisors in presenting languages as living, vital keys to culture. Language teachers by the thousands attended summer institutes in order to learn new methods, and returned to their students in the fall with a contagious enthusiasm and an increased effectiveness.

Some critics of the NDEA pointed out that America was not really interested in the humanistic value of language study when the federal government equated such study with national defense. This was equating language with "ordinance," and we needed "to pass the ammunition," they said. The validity of this criticism cannot be determined at this time. In this writer's opinion, however, even though the National Defense Education Act may have been prompted by "materialistic considerations," the very fact that it was passed and did give such positive encouragement to modern language study may result, in the long run, as one of the great advances made in the humanities during the twentieth century.

CHAPTER VI

Audio-Visual Aids

After World War II, increased use of audio-visual aids in language teaching resulted from the perfecting of some older materials, together with the development of new techniques and new media which facilitated and made more effective their use. Language records had been used for years to bring songs, conversational dialogues, literary selections, phonetic drills, and intonation patterns into the classroom. Language conversation courses on records had been used for a long time by commercial language schools, and are still widely sold.[1] Maps, posters, travel pictures, films, slides, and many other types of realia have had a long history of use.

However, until the Armed Services made extensive use of records in World War II to present linguistic patterns, allowing the students time to repeat each pattern given, the "audio" half of audio-visual aids was not an integrated part of language instruction. Once the structural patterns of foreign languages were scientifically determined by linguists and recorded by native speakers on disks or magnetic tapes, language teachers were in a better position to give the students the quantity and quality of ear training which they needed as they began new language study. Since the audio-lingual method began with listening comprehension, the use of the language laboratory, one of the newest and best of the audio aids, will be discussed first.

The Language Laboratory [2]

Linguistic scientists agree that the correct approach to learning a new language is (1) through much listening to the foreign sounds and (2) through repeated practice in speaking them. The language laboratory is admirably suited for this approach, because it gives

---

1 For a listing of the many commercial companies which sell language records, see William R. Parker, *The National Interest and Foreign Languages,* p. 117.

2 For techniques on the use of language laboratories, see Edward M. Stack, *The Language Laboratory and Modern Language Teaching* (New York: Oxford University Press, 1960).

the student the opportunity to be an active "hearer and doer of the word." Much time spent in attentive listening leads to understanding the spoken sounds; much regular imitation of these sounds leads to fluency. The individual student in the usual type of classroom does not have enough opportunity to hear and speak the new language. The language laboratory multiplies his opportunities.

A language laboratory is, in simple terms, any mechanical or electro-mechanical device which transmits recorded or "live" speech to a listener, and which affords the listener a chance to practice the sounds heard.[3] A more effective type of laboratory is one which gives the student a sense of privacy while he hears and speaks the new sounds. Earphones alone, plugged into a record player or into a more elaborate source, can give this feeling; earphones and a student booth afford still greater isolation. If the earphones are connected through the device to those of his teacher so that the latter can hear and monitor him, the student's potential for learning is greatly increased. When the student uses materials recorded by a native speaker, or by one of near-native ability, he finds that the language laboratory will aid him in the following ways:

1. He always hears the authentic language. In the classroom a student's peer usually gives him a weak version of the foreign language when the teacher asks him to read aloud. In the laboratory the student gets the correct pronunciation and the correct intonation at the same time.

2. The student early accustoms himself to the normal speed of the native speaker. In the usual classroom the teacher tends to slow down his speed in using the foreign language in an effort to make all students understand him. Later, when the student hears a native speaker using his language at normal tempo, he will say that the foreigner speaks too fast.

3. The laboratory gives the student much opportunity to hear a variety of voices correctly speaking the foreign language, and the student can practice the sounds for an entire period, if he wishes. The regular classroom offers one model at first: the teacher; and little time can be given for individual practice.

---

[3] For help on planning and equipping a language laboratory, consult Joseph C. Hutchinson, *Modern Foreign Languages in the High School: The Language Laboratory*, United States Office of Education Bulletin 1961, No. 23 (Washington, D.C.: United States Government Printing Office, 1961).

4. A teacher can listen in while a student is practicing sound patterns, and can give immediate, individual help to the student without other students knowing about it.

5. By comparing his pronunciation with that of his model, the student can know immediately what his errors are, and he can correct them.

6. A variety of materials can be presented. After the student has mastered the basic sound patterns, he can add interpretative nuances to his oral practice by listening to native speakers read poetry, dramas, or selected passages from novels or short stories. Improvement in diction results, as well as a growing appreciation of the foreign literature.

Laboratories reinforce language learning. Maximum effectiveness of the language laboratory occurs when its use supplements and enlarges classroom language study. Dialogues or pattern drills already used in the classroom should be reviewed and varied in numerous exercises designed especially for the laboratory. Many of the new, beginning texts for use in junior and senior high schools and in colleges are accompanied by records or tapes for use in the laboratory. Such integrated language programs for secondary schools are the A-LM French, German, Italian, Russian, and Spanish series published by Harcourt, Brace & World, Inc.[4]

Laboratory in the home. In many homes there are record players; in a few there are tape recorders. Additional practice of foreign language patterns can be provided in any home which has a record player or a magnetic tape recorder. Some of the lessons of the integrated programs used in schools can be carried home on disk or tape for homework practice. A profusion of additional disks and tapes for language practice is offered by numerous companies.[5]

Laboratories bring problems. The presence of a language laboratory in an educational institution can be a great asset to language learning; it also can be a liability if poorly equipped and unimaginatively used. Some of the problems connected with the installation and use of the laboratory are: (1) selection and maintenance of technical equipment, (2) preparation of materials compatible with

---

[4] For extensive listings of similar programs for elementary and secondary schools and for colleges, consult the section "Integrated Programs" of the Modern Language Association's *Selective List of Materials* (1962).

[5] Consult the MLA's *Selective List of Materials.*

the objectives of the language course, (3) scheduling of laboratory use, (4) integration of laboratory and classroom, and (5) the excessive demand on hearing for some students.

Great care must go into the selection of high-quality technical equipment for the laboratory so that language sounds can be transmitted and received clearly. For example, a poorly wired console or faulty headphones can negate the effectiveness of the laboratory. Teachers usually do not have the time or experience to serve as laboratory maintenance personnel; therefore, the school or college has the added problem of getting someone else to service or repair equipment. If tape recorders and taped programs can be located in a central library, and if only a headset, microphone, and operational switches are actually present in student booths, maintenance problems can be reduced considerably.

A problem greater than that of equipment is the selection and preparation of materials for the laboratory. If the primary aim of the course is to teach students to understand and speak a foreign language, the beginning materials must be completely oral, starting with exercises on pronunciation, and without reference to the printed word at any time during the first few weeks. There must be numerous pattern drills available for the students, and they must be varied enough in nature to maintain the student's active interest.

In regard to scheduling laboratory use there must be the following decisions: (1) whether to schedule a complete class at the same hour for laboratory practice, or (2) to set up the laboratory for individual student use on a library-type basis. If the secondary school system is large, scheduling by whole classes may present some problems as language teachers try to avoid conflicts with schedules for lunches, buses, and special school functions.

Integrating the laboratory drills with classroom activities is another serious problem. Gustave Mathieu [6] gives excellent advice on this subject in a paper "Recommendations on the Learnings Which Should Occur in the Language Laboratory and in the Classroom," written for a conference held in New York City on November 27 and 28, 1960. A summary of his advice follows:

---

[6] Conference on the College Language Laboratory, *Publications of the Language Laboratory*, Vol. V (Ann Arbor, Mich.: University of Michigan, 1961), pp. 58–95.

SUMMARY IN DO'S AND DON'T'S FOR LANGUAGE LAB PRACTICE [7]

1. Use only materials intended for oral communication.

2. Whatever the learner says should be a complete utterance and in the target language.

3. Each lab period should preferably include listening-comprehension, creative pattern practice and mimicry-memorization practice.

4. When the learner is required to "respond," always provide the correct response for self-correction.

5. Each exercise within each practice should be no longer than five minutes.

6. Visual clues and pictorial stimuli are of great value as long as they do not contain any writing.

7. Do not let the learner see in written form what he is hearing until he has mastered it by ear alone.

8. Never let the learner say anything in the beginning stages unless he has had ample opportunity of hearing it first.

9. All materials for creative pattern practice should first be presented in class.

10. Do not devote more than a very small fraction of the lab time to self-evaluation (record and playback).

Visual Materials

The use of visual materials in all stages of language learning reinforces the learning process by adding the sense of sight to that of sound. Many persons, especially adolescents and adults, learn faster through the eye than through the ear. Visual aids serve to convey concepts immediately to the learner of a foreign language, shortening or bypassing the association with similar concepts in the mother tongue. The use of visual aids serves best in the classroom as a technique to add vocabulary and knowledge of culture; the language laboratory serves best in linguistic aspects.

In the beginning stages, on all levels, the teacher is exhibit number one. By pointing to himself he can teach names for parts of the body; by pointing to objects in the classroom, he teaches more nouns and adjectives; through gestures, facial expressions, and other aspects of acting, verbal concepts are conveyed. Maps, posters, and pictures of all types serve to increase vocabulary content and cul-

---

[7] *Ibid.*, pp. 91–92. For "A Dozen Do's and Don't's" in connection with planning and operating a language laboratory or an electronic classroom in a high school, see pages 109–110.

tural understanding. All the while, the teacher repeatedly gives the foreign equivalents for the item or concept presented, and the students repeat the sounds until they learn them.[8]

Films, filmstrips, and slides. Motion picture films, with or without sound, serve to give knowledge of "culture in action." Films with sound tracks are used in advanced stages of language study to increase and test aural comprehension as well.

Filmstrips and slides lend themselves better to classroom teaching because the pictures presented can be held for as long as desired for conversation or drill, and the sequence of presentation can be controlled by the teacher or students. Integrated audio-visual teaching programs based on filmstrips or color slides are available in America and in Europe.[9] The Department of Audio-Visual Education of Wayne State University in Detroit, for example, has produced a beginning French course, *Images de France,* based on 1,200 color slides, with accompanying magnetic tapes. The MLA *Selective List of Materials* lists many additional sets.

Language Teaching by Television

A comparatively new medium for language teaching is television: open-circuit (broadcast to the public), and closed-circuit (telecasts confined to one building or to buildings connected by special cables). Most of the TV language teaching to date has been done over open-circuit stations. The Joint Council on Educational TV published in August, 1959, a partial listing of language courses taught on 41 educational and 32 commercial TV stations, plus a few closed-circuit courses in high schools and colleges.[10] Since 1952 the Federal Communications Commission has reserved 275 TV channels for educational use; but at the end of 1961, only 62 were in use.

Elementary schools have made the most use of TV for class instruction in languages. In 1960–61, 7,500 elementary schools

---

[8] For a full treatment of teaching techniques, consult Theodore Huebener, *Audio-Visual Techniques in Teaching Foreign Languages* (New York: New York University Press, 1960).

[9] Education Clearing House, "A Bibliography on the Teaching of Modern Languages," in *Educational Studies and Documents,* 1955, No. 13 (Paris: United Nations Educational, Scientific and Cultural Organization, 1955), Chapter IV, pp. 61–68.

[10] See William R. Parker, *The National Interest and Foreign Languages,* p. 66.

were offering some TV teaching to an estimated 3,500,000 children.[11] Most of the schools were receiving French or Spanish lessons, with a few scattered telecasts of other languages. In many of these schools there was a shortage of elementary teachers qualified to teach foreign languages, and the televised lessons made language offerings possible in those schools. The regular classroom teachers often took part in the TV drills along with their pupils, later supplementing their own work in language by taking night or Saturday classes in teaching methods.

Televised language courses for credit were offered by 250 colleges and universities to approximately 250,000 students in 1960–61. Often a college would permit some of its students to take by TV a course which it did not offer in its regular curriculum. Many high schools likewise permitted such practice.

Closed-circuit television has been used successfully to teach foreign languages in college. A good teacher presents structural patterns of the language to large numbers of students who are scattered around in several other rooms of the building in front of TV screens. Student assistants in those rooms direct the language students in drills or exercises presented by the TV teacher. A two-way hookup between TV studio and classrooms makes it possible for the teacher to call on individual students in any room, if he wishes. These large groups are usually broken up into small "quiz groups" two or three times a week so that instructors can test the individual student's progress.

In teacher-preparatory programs, future teachers in rooms separate from the televised classroom can observe a televised language class in action. The language supervisor can call the observers' attention to special techniques being used in the teaching while the lesson is in progress, without disturbing the pupils who are being taught. This use of TV to demonstrate techniques of teaching is one of its finest.

Colleges also send language programs by closed-circuit TV to other schools which are connected to them by cable. In this way, college teachers can extend language training to elementary or high schools in their area, or to other colleges.

---

11 J. Richard Reid, "An Exploratory Survey of Foreign Language Teaching by Television in the United States," in *Reports of Surveys and Studies in the Teaching of Modern Foreign Languages* (New York: Modern Language Association, 1961), p. 197.

Potentialities of television language teaching. With school and college populations increasing faster than the production of classrooms and teaching staff, expansion of educational television in the United States is inevitable; and language lessons through this medium likewise will increase. The extended use will probably take two directions: formal and informal. The formal will include regular lessons telecast to students on all academic levels and for credit; the informal will be noncredit courses designed primarily for adults.

Formal use of TV will integrate the televised lessons with the students' use of the language laboratory. For the language teacher, in-service, formal extension courses in methods of teaching can be telecast into the teacher's home, thus removing the problem of commuting to some academic center for such instruction. In rural sections, as well as in scattered suburban areas, the distance to academic centers keeps many teachers from getting the immediate help which they need.

Opportunities for adults to continue learning in post-high school or college years is a growing need in America. Informal use of educational television will include language lessons for adults. The informal programs will be of several types: (1) refresher courses in languages previously studied, (2) conversation courses for purposes of travel to some foreign area, and (3) basic beginning language courses for personal pleasure.

There are 2,200 existing television channels, 275 of which are reserved for educational television, and only 62 of the 275 in use. It is obvious that when state legislatures and departments of education become aware of the ways in which educational television can meet the needs for more formal and informal instruction, the use of this medium will increase sharply. The National Association of Educational Broadcasters estimates that a total of 1,197 channels (instead of 275) are needed in the United States, if adequate coverage is to be given.[12]

MLA survey of foreign language teaching by television. Under a special commission from the Modern Language Association, J. Richard Reid in 1961 surveyed foreign language teaching by television in the United States. His five recommendations were: (1) there should be a clearing house of information concerning

---

[12] National Association of Educational Broadcasters, *The Needs of Education for Television Channel Allocations,* United States Office of Education, OE–34017 (Washington, D.C.: United States Government Printing Office, 1962).

TV teaching, located in one national agency; (2) television teachers and producers need help from a national corps of consultants, as well as a national fund to subsidize intervisitation among TV teachers of foreign languages, if the present isolation in which most TV teachers and producers work is to end; (3) producers of TV courses in adjacent areas should consider combining resources in order to offer more language teaching at less cost; (4) there should be more use of video-tape recordings so that good language teaching can be recorded for subsequent use; and (5) there should be a more extensive survey of the whole field of language teaching by television.

Professor Reid concluded his survey as follows:

> . . . A single, skillful, inspired teacher, on a city-wide or nation-wide network, can not and will not be able to do the work of several hundred, or a hundred, classroom teachers—or of one classroom teacher. Such a television teacher can, however, do a significant part of the work of several hundred teachers.
>
> Television is not *the answer* to the shortage of teachers, but insofar as TV teaching of foreign languages is done by skillful, inspired teachers, backed by sound advice from linguists and producers, and by a sound program in the schools, television can be a *major part* of the solution to this problem. The virtue is not in the TV tube or in any one person in the studio. It is in all the people who collaborate in its use.[13]

The Teaching Machine

Experimentation and research are in progress on the use of automated teaching systems for programmed language courses. In this new "step-increment" learning system, a foreign language is broken down into thousands of short, habit-forming responses or steps. These are arranged in a predetermined sequence, tape-recorded, and given to the machine, which presents them one at a time, letting the student know the correct answer a moment after he has responded. In its "News and Reports" of research projects under Title VII, the United States Office of Education has listed periodically such projects. *The Christian Science Monitor* reported in two

---

[13] J. Richard Reid, "An Exploratory Survey of Foreign Language Teaching by Television in the United States," in *Reports of Surveys and Studies in the Teaching of Modern Foreign Languages,* p. 207.

articles (February 10 and February 24, 1962) an experiment at the University of Michigan where a graduate student had studied a programmed course in Spanish for 215 hours before going to Mexico to practice speaking the language with Mexicans. He stayed in Mexico two weeks, talked to Mexicans, got their answers, and tape-recorded the whole experiment by means of a tape recorder which he carried around his neck. When the student returned to the University of Michigan, Professor E. Rand Morton, who had programmed the course for the experiment, analyzed the tapes and found that the student had a Spanish-language proficiency of a twelve-year-old Mexican boy.

The excellent results of the Michigan experiment seem to prophesy much future use of the "teaching machine" by individuals who prefer to follow a self-instructional program rather than the mass-production type. Some very brilliant students might prefer to use the programmed approach in order to learn a foreign language fast; other students who must take more time for their learning could pace themselves according to their abilities. If each type of student can achieve language proficiency by using a programmed course as a supplement to regular instruction, the language teacher will have gained a most valuable audio-visual aid.[14]

---

[14] For reports of research on the teaching machine, as well as bibliography on major aspects of language teaching, consult Howard L. Nostrand, *et al., Research on Language Teaching: An Annotated International Bibliography for 1945–61* (Seattle, Wash.: University of Washington Press, 1962).

CHAPTER VII

Preparation of Modern Foreign
Language Teachers

Before 1955. Teachers of modern foreign languages in the United States received very little preparation for teaching until the late nineteenth century. Many of the early teachers of French and German were immigrants who taught in private schools. They usually were fluent speakers of the languages they taught, but often their teaching technique was poor, according to reports later published by some of their students. After the Civil War, with the expansion of the public elementary and secondary schools to accommodate the throngs of immigrants' children, city school systems found native teachers hard to obtain, and they began to establish training courses for local persons who wanted to teach languages.

German teachers were in short supply for the public elementary schools of several large Midwestern cities after 1870. Cincinnati and a few other cities tried to alleviate the teacher shortage by introducing German courses into their training schools. A German-American Teachers Seminary was established in Milwaukee in 1878. In 1880, the University of Michigan began a one-semester course for teachers of French, and in 1883 started one for German teachers. The University of Wisconsin began a pedagogical seminary for German teachers in 1887, and the University of Kansas introduced methods courses for teachers of German in 1890. The above-mentioned universities (Michigan, Wisconsin, and Kansas) were the only ones which gave some attention to teacher training in their regular sessions by 1890. It is understandable why the Committee of Ten, appointed by the NEA in 1892, in its report of 1893 made the following statement: "The worst obstacle to the progress of modern language study is the lack of properly equipped teachers. There seems to be at present no institution where persons intending to teach German, French or Spanish in our elementary or secondary schools can receive the special preparation they need." [1]

By 1900, teacher-training courses in modern foreign languages were offered to upperclassmen (and in a few institutions to graduate students) at the following places: University of Illinois, University of Nebraska, Cornell University, University of Chicago, Columbia University and Teachers College, University of Minnesota, and Mount Holyoke College. By 1927, there were 347 modern language departments in the United States which offered teacher training in languages, according to a survey by a committee of the Modern Foreign Language Study. In 1959, 758 institutions of higher learning reported on a Modern Language Association survey that they offered enough training in modern foreign languages to certify teachers in their respective states.

Summer school programs to train modern language teachers were started by Lambert Sauveur at Amherst College in 1877. Dr. Sauveur, an advocate of the "natural" method of teaching modern foreign languages, had come to the United States from Belgium around 1870 to join Professor Theophilus Heness, a German, who had established a private school of modern foreign languages in New Haven in 1866. Professors Heness and Sauveur were vigorous proponents of the "natural" way of learning a foreign language, and between 1884 and 1894 they taught in summer language programs in several Eastern colleges. Dr. Sauveur taught in Rockford, Illinois, in the summer of 1893.

Middlebury College started a summer language program for German teachers in 1912, one for French in 1916, and one for Spanish in 1917. Mount Holyoke College began a summer program for German teachers in 1927. Other centers for summer study of languages soon developed, such as the Cleveland School of Modern Languages, and the school at Pennsylvania State College. Several colleges initiated summer and academic-year study abroad, and others established language houses and language clubs to benefit future teachers. After 1959, the summer institutes established by the National Defense Education Act offered in-service training to thousands of modern foreign language teachers (see Chapter V).

---

[1] E. W. Bagster-Collins, "History of Modern Language Teaching in the United States," in *Studies in Modern Language Teaching* (New York: The Macmillan Company, 1930), p. 76.

Teacher preparation after 1955. The first major step toward creating standards for admission of teachers into a modern foreign language profession was the statement on "Qualifications for Secondary School Teachers of Modern Foreign Languages," issued by a steering committee of the Modern Language Association in February, 1955. A second step toward this concept of profession was taken in June, 1960, when the MLA Proficiency Tests for Teachers and Advanced Students were used for the first time to measure the qualifications established five years earlier. These two steps, taken by the Modern Language Association in the interest of improving modern language teaching in the secondary schools, determined the direction which teacher preparation would take in undergraduate academic programs.

Qualifications for secondary school teachers. Starting with the basic assumption that a foreign language teacher should be a person of good character who has received a well-balanced education plus the "appropriate training in professional education, psychology, and secondary school methods," the MLA statement of 1955 offered the following specific criteria for minimal, good, and superior competencies: [2]

1. AURAL UNDERSTANDING

Minimal. The ability to get the sense of what an educated native says when he is enunciating carefully and speaking simply on a general subject.

Good. The ability to understand conversation at average tempo, lectures, and news broadcasts.

Superior. The ability to follow closely and with ease all types of standard speech, such as rapid or group conversation, plays, and movies.

Test.[3] These abilities can be tested by dictations, by the Listening Comprehension Tests of the College Entrance Board—thus far developed for French, German, Italian, Russian, and Spanish—or by similar tests for these and other languages, with an extension in range and difficulty for the superior level.

2. SPEAKING

Minimal. The ability to talk on prepared topics (e.g., for classroom

---

[2] Modern Language Association, "Qualifications for Secondary School Teachers of Modern Foreign Languages," *PMLA,* LXX, No. 4, Part 2 (September, 1955), 46–49.

[3] The "MLA Proficiency Tests for Teachers and Advanced Students" are now available for all seven areas of competency.

situations) without obvious faltering, and to use the common expressions needed for getting around in the foreign country, speaking with a pronunciation readily understandable to a native.

Good. The ability to talk with a native without making glaring mistakes, and with a command of vocabulary and syntax sufficient to express one's thoughts in sustained conversation. This implies speech at normal speed with good pronunciation and intonation.

Superior. The ability to approximate native speech in vocabulary, intonation, and pronunciation (e.g., the ability to exchange ideas and to be at ease in social situations).

Test. For the present, this ability has to be tested by interview or by a recorded set of questions with a blank disc or tape for recording answers.

3. READING

Minimal. The ability to grasp directly (i.e., without translating) the meaning of simple, nontechnical prose, except for an occasional word.

Good. The ability to read with immediate comprehension prose and verse of average difficulty and mature content.

Superior. The ability to read, almost as easily as in English, material of considerable difficulty, such as essays and literary criticism.

Test. These abilities can be tested by a graded series of timed reading passages, with comprehension questions and multiple-choice or free-response answers.

4. WRITING

Minimal. The ability to write correctly sentences or paragraphs such as would be developed orally for classroom situations, and the ability to write a short, simple letter.

Good. The ability to write a simple "free composition" with clarity and correctness in vocabulary, idiom, and syntax.

Superior. The ability to write on a variety of subjects with idiomatic naturalness, ease of expression, and some feeling for the style of the language.

Test. These abilities can be tested by multiple-choice syntax items, dictations, translation of English sentences or paragraphs, and a controlled letter or free composition.

5. LANGUAGE ANALYSIS

Minimal. A working command of the sound patterns and grammar patterns of the foreign language, and a knowledge of its main differences from English.

Good. A basic knowledge of the historical development and present characteristics of the language, and an awareness of the difference between the language as spoken and as written.

Superior. Ability to apply knowledge of descriptive, comparative, and historical linguistics to the language-teaching situation.

Test. Such information and insight can be tested for levels 1 and 2 by multiple-choice and free-response items on pronunciation, intonation patterns, and syntax; for levels 2 and 3, items on philology and descriptive linguistics.

6. CULTURE

Minimal. An awareness of language as an essential element among the learned and shared experiences that combine to form a particular culture, and a rudimentary knowledge of the geography, history, literature, art, social customs, and contemporary civilization of the foreign people.

Good. First-hand knowledge of some literary masterpieces, and understanding of the principal ways in which the foreign culture resembles and differs from our own, and possession of an organized body of information on the foreign people and their civilization.

Superior. An enlightened understanding of the foreign people and their culture, achieved through personal contact, preferably by travel and residence abroad; through study of systematic descriptions of the foreign culture; and through study of literature and the arts.

Test. Such information and insight can be tested by multiple-choice literary and cultural acquaintance tests for levels 1 and 2; for level 3, written comments on passages of prose or poetry that discuss or reveal significant aspects of the foreign culture.

7. PROFESSIONAL PREPARATION

(Note the final paragraph of the prefatory statement.)

Minimal. Some knowledge of effective methods and techniques of language teaching.

Good. The ability to apply knowledge of methods and techniques to the teaching situation (e.g., audio-visual techniques) and to relate one's teaching of the language to other areas of the curriculum.

Superior. A mastery of recognized teaching methods, and the ability to experiment with and evaluate new methods and techniques.

Test. Such knowledge and ability can be tested by multiple-choice answers to questions on pedagogy and language-teaching methods, plus written comment on language-teaching situations.

Qualifications immediately endorsed. By 1956, the MLA statement of qualifications had been endorsed by 18 language organizations of regional and national scope, and was given wide publicity through journals of these organizations. Likewise, the publishing of these competencies in *The Bulletin of the National Association of Secondary School Principals,* November, 1955, made them known to a large audience outside the language teachers' organizations. On local and state levels, however, changes in teacher preparation were slow in coming.

State Certification Requirements

As late as June 1960, all State Departments of Education in the United States based certification to teach modern foreign languages on credit-hours in the languages concerned, plus a certain number of required hours in professional education courses. The hours required in language varied from 12 to 36, with the biggest number of states (20) requiring 24 hours. In several states as many as six hours could be applied from previous high school study of the language. In no state were the audio-lingual proficiencies of a teacher requisites for teaching languages in elementary and secondary schools. The state certification boards had given the responsibility for testing and certifying these proficiencies to the local institutions which prepared the teachers.

There was no significant trend in the states toward increasing the credit-hours required for certification. However, of 22 cities in 13 states and the District of Columbia which set their own standards, 12 exceeded the foreign language requirements set for certification by their states.[4] Some states were experimenting with proficiency tests in the pedagogical preparation of teachers, but such tests could not yet be extended to the modern foreign language field. Pennsylvania was the first state to use the MLA Foreign Language Proficiency Tests for Teachers and Advanced Students when on January 26, 1962, the State Department of Education administered them to test the proficiency and teaching ability of native speakers of the foreign languages who were candidates for certification. Other states, no doubt, will make similar use of these tests, since national norms were established in 1961.

Undergraduate Preparation for Secondary School Modern Language Teachers [5]

Undergraduate preparation of modern foreign language teachers is divided into two categories: academic (subject-matter courses)

---

[4] Anna Balakian, "Certification Requirements for Modern Foreign Language Teachers," *PMLA,* LXXVI, No. 2 (May, 1961), 20–35.

[5] For extensive treatment of this theme, see Marjorie C. Johnston, ed., *Modern Foreign Languages in the High School,* U.S. Department of Health, Education, and Welfare, OE–27005 (Washington, D.C.: United States Government Printing Office, 1958).

and professional (educational psychology, methods, practice teaching). Most of the modern foreign language teachers are prepared in liberal arts colleges and in private and state colleges and universities. Teachers colleges, rapidly disappearing from the American educational scene, prepare few language teachers. In many colleges of all types, however, programs of teacher preparation fall short of meeting the qualifications established by the Modern Language Association.

Language preparation. Following the pattern set by state certification boards, the colleges and universities based their teacher-preparation programs on credit-hours in language and pedagogy rather than on proficiencies demonstrated in those areas. Courses to develop the audio-lingual skills needed by future secondary school teachers were neglected in many colleges; up to 75 per cent of the students' course load could be in literature, much of which was taught in English. Up to 1962, there was no consistent policy of testing the students' proficiency in speaking the foreign language before admitting them to the teacher-preparation program in language. Many students with deficiencies in some of the language skills were allowed to carry their weaknesses throughout their college training and into their classrooms.

In order to improve the present status of teacher preparation in the modern languages, Committee I of the Northeast Conference presented to the 1961 meeting the following recommendations: [6]

1. Superior high school and college foreign language students should be encouraged to become teachers. More government scholarships or loans should be made available for students who enter the teacher-preparatory program.

2. The linguistic competence of prospective foreign language teachers ought to be tested at three periods: (a) upon entrance into college, (b) at the end of the junior year, and (c) toward the end of the senior year. The Modern Language Association Foreign Language Proficiency Tests for Teachers and Advanced Students might well be used to indicate whether the teacher candidate had reached a minimal, good, or superior level of proficiency.

3. The language trainee should understand that there are seven areas of competence: listening comprehension, speaking, reading, writing,

---

[6] Northeast Conference on the Teaching of Foreign Languages, ed. Seymour L. Flaxman, *Modern Language Teaching in School and College* (Princeton, N.J.: Princeton University Press, 1961), pp. 26–27. Copyright 1961, Northeast Conference on the Teaching of Foreign Languages. Reprinted by permission.

applied linguistics, culture-civilization, and professional preparation. Subject-matter courses should be planned to fit the needs of the prospective teachers, as these needs relate to the seven areas. Some students are fluent speakers and writers of a foreign language, yet are weak in language analysis, literature, or culture. They should be permitted to omit courses in which they already have adequate proficiency, in order to concentrate on other areas where they have less proficiency.

4. Colleges must provide language courses built upon high school programs that have audio-lingual instruction.

5. A well-balanced specialized program of language courses should be provided. This program must go beyond the intermediate college level and become a substantial college major, including courses leading to competence in all seven areas. In addition, study abroad is recommended for the junior year, or for the summer at the end of the junior year.

Professional Preparation[7]

Students preparing to teach modern foreign languages usually take courses in the principles of teaching and learning, in the psychology of adolescence, and in teaching methods. In addition, they usually teach for a period of time under supervision of a "master teacher" or a foreign language supervisor. Many of the colleges have eliminated the methods course as such, incorporating "methods" into the total practice-teaching experience. In some instances the foreign language supervisors supply the practice teachers adequate information on methods and materials; however, such help is almost completely lacking in many other cases unless it is presented in an organized course. In order to insure that each practice teacher has such professional help before his practice teaching experience, Committee I recommended the following to the 1961 Northeast Conference: [8]

> 2.3. During the junior year, or at the latest in the first term of the senior year, the prospective teacher must enroll in a course on methods of teaching foreign languages. It is the responsibility of the language department to assure that such a course is offered.

---

[7] See Wesley Childers, Barbara Bell, and Harry Margulis, "Teacher Education Curricula in the Modern Foreign Languages," in *Reports of Surveys and Studies in the Teaching of Modern Foreign Languages* (New York: Modern Language Association, 1961), Chapter IX, pp. 153–64.

[8] Northeast Conference, *op. cit.,* pp. 27–28. Copyright 1961, Northeast Conference on the Teaching of Foreign Languages. Reprinted by permission.

2.4. The course on methods must include the following:

1. Objectives of foreign language instruction.

2. Modern classroom procedures.

3. Use of materials involved in the current and approved presentation of foreign languages.

4. Preparation of tests.

5. Use of a laboratory.

6. Discussion of and familiarity with professional organizations and publications.

7. Observation of classes in action.

2.5. For the practice teaching experience, each student teacher should be assigned to a master teacher who uses the approved methods and techniques. Throughout the period of practice teaching, the instructor in methods must be allotted time, at regular intervals, to visit and supervise each student teacher on the job and to arrange evaluation conferences with the student teacher and the critic teacher.

There is a growing practice in colleges and universities of having a committee on teacher preparation, composed of specialists from the Department of Education and the language department concerned, guide a prospective language teacher throughout his training period. Committee I of the Northeast Conference recommended a similar plan:

2.2. Each foreign language major who intends to teach should be assigned, not later than the beginning of the junior year, to an adviser specializing in teacher training. It would be the duty of the adviser, through frequent conferences with each student and the teaching personnel in the foreign language department, to aid in determining whether the student is suited in temperament, competences, and scholarship to teach. Students who do not so qualify should be advised to withdraw from the program.[9]

Preparation of College and University Teachers

Little attention was given in the first 60 years of the twentieth century to the training of language majors for college teaching. The graduate schools in an effort to develop scholars overlooked the fact that almost 100 per cent of their language majors became teachers after they received the M.A. or Ph.D. degrees. Many grad-

---

[9] Northeast Conference (1961), *op. cit.*, p. 27. Since the present writer was one of the five authors of Committee I's recommendations, and since these still represent his point of view, he has cited them at length.

uate schools turned over first- and second-year college language classes to teaching assistants, without giving them any training in teaching methods, or any supervision while they were teaching. These assistants, who formed 12 per cent of the total number of college and university language teachers in 1959–60, were teaching basic language courses while their main work in graduate school was concentrated on literature.[10]

Recognizing that present practices in graduate schools do not adequately prepare the scholar-teacher for the type of language teaching he would do, Committee II of the Northeast Conference in 1961 recommended a new approach to graduate training, whose chief features would be: [11]

1. A carefully planned, three-year graduate program, guided throughout by a senior member of the language department concerned.

2. The first year of graduate study would determine the student's competency in understanding, speaking, reading, and writing the language, devoting about 25 per cent of his first-year program to these aspects; three-fourths of the student's program could be devoted to literature, or linguistics, or philology.

3. In the second year the graduate student would teach a beginning or a second-year class throughout the year, while continuing his course work. He would be guided and supervised in every detail of his teaching by his adviser.

4. During the third year, the student could teach two undergraduate classes, one of which would be on the same level of the preceding year. In addition, while preparing for his examinations, he would take an interdepartmental seminar which would help him integrate knowledge gained from all his courses.

5. The student would be paid for teaching the three language courses, the payments to be spread equally over the three years of graduate study.

Post-Graduate Training

Elementary and secondary school language teachers have been

---

[10] See Mara Vamos and John Harmon, "Modern Foreign Language Faculties in Colleges and Universities," in *Reports of Surveys and Studies in the Teaching of Modern Foreign Languages,* Chapter VIII, p. 144.

[11] Summarized from the Northeast Conference (1961), *op. cit.,* pp. 36–39.

given much help by National Defense Education Act Language Institutes in developing their audio-lingual proficiencies (see Chapter V). Likewise, in-service training courses established by state language supervisors or by colleges have given needed information on effective teaching methods to these teachers. Numerous grants are available to teachers on all levels for travel and study abroad.[12] Also, many colleges and universities sponsor study abroad; [13] and in recent years some universities have established study programs of many types in foreign lands.[14] The Mutual Education and Cultural Exchange Act of 1961, passed by Congress as a broadening of the Fulbright and Smith-Mundt Acts, authorized the financing of foreign travel for United States language teachers.

The obvious need at present is for National Defense Education Act Language Institutes (or for similar types) devoted to the retraining of college teachers in the use of audio-lingual materials and methods. During the first five years of the NDEA, no institutes for college teachers had been held. If such help on a national level is not provided in the near future, graduates from the better secondary schools will lose their aural-oral competencies in modern foreign languages while they are students in college. Many prospective foreign language teachers will become disinterested in their language courses because of the inadequacies of their teachers, and will drop out of teacher-preparatory programs. Loss of a considerable number of potential teachers at this time would be a severe blow to the profession, since it already needs about twice as many new language teachers as are graduating annually from American colleges and universities.

---

[12] See UNESCO, *Study Abroad* (Paris: UNESCO, 1961).

[13] See John A. Garraty and Walter Adams, *From Main Street to the Left Bank: Students and Scholars Abroad* (East Lansing, Mich.: Michigan State University Press, 1959).

[14] See Edward W. Weidner, *The World Role of Universities* (New York: McGraw-Hill Book Company, 1962).

CHAPTER VIII

A Decade of Progress: 1952-1962

Viewed against the background of the first half of the twentieth century, the progress made in foreign language teaching and learning in the United States during the decade 1952–62 was phenomenal. Shortly before the renaissance of interest in foreign languages started in 1952, languages seemed to be experiencing their darkest hours. Lessons of America's linguistic unpreparedness during World War II and in the Korean War appeared to have been forgotten. Language teachers, disheartened by falling enrollments and by the apathy of their students toward the conventional teaching methods, blamed their "doom" on the educationists. Common ground for cooperation could not be seen by either group. Then after May, 1952, the situation suddenly changed, revealing that many people and many forces in American society were deeply concerned about the study of foreign languages.

After 1952: men, money, and a foreign language program. Two men—Earl J. McGrath, United States Commissioner of Education, and William R. Parker, General Secretary of the Modern Language Association—and a Rockefeller Foundation grant were largely responsible for the sudden, dramatic change in 1952 from a negative to a positive attitude toward foreign languages. The national conference which Commissioner McGrath called in Washington in January, 1953, initiated the more active role which the United States Office of Education was to play in support of foreign languages during the following decade. In June, 1952, William Parker announced that the Rockefeller Foundation had made a grant of $120,000 to the Modern Language Association for a three-year study of the role foreign languages and literatures should play in American life. This grant was increased by $115,000 in 1954 and extended for three more years.

The Executive Council of the Modern Language Association set up a Foreign Language Program in the spring of 1952, formulated broad policies concerning its operation, and appointed William

Parker to be its director.[1] In December, 1952, the Council appointed a steering committee of eleven persons to advise the director. Parker's imaginative leadership and his cogent presentation of the status of foreign language study in terms of national needs had immediate results.[2] National conferences brought together language teachers and professional educators to discuss ways of improving foreign language teaching; surveys of the language enrollments in elementary and secondary schools gave significant data on the current language situation; studies of the qualifications desired in modern foreign language teachers were made; and policy statements on many aspects of language learning and teaching were formulated. The MLA's free "List of Available Materials" indicates the scope of activities completed by the Association under William Parker and his successor, George Winchester Stone, Jr.

Support from the United States Office of Education. The recent work of the United States Office of Education in the interest of modern foreign language instruction—begun in January, 1953, at the McGrath Conference in Washington—became active after 1956. In July, 1956, the Office of Education appointed Marjorie C. Johnston as its first permanent Staff Specialist in Foreign Languages. In 1957 the Office of Education sponsored two conferences in Washington: (1) For 20 Government agencies, called in March by the Commissioner of Education, before which William Parker appeared and presented data on the status of modern foreign languages; (2) A conference in May on "Modern Foreign Languages in the High School," at which specialists emphasized the increased need for foreign languages, the new objectives and techniques in teaching, and the preparation of foreign language teachers.[3]

Data presented to these conferences were made available to Congressional committees which were seeking to strengthen the teaching of science, mathematics, and foreign languages in American schools. After the National Defense Education Act became law in September, 1958, the Office of Education was charged with

---

[1] Directors of the MLA's Foreign Language Program (1952–62) were: William Parker (1952–56), Theodore Andersson (1956–58), Kenneth Mildenberger (1958–59), Archibald MacAllister (January–July 1959), and Donald Walsh (since July, 1959).

[2] The first edition of Parker's *The National Interest and Foreign Languages* appeared in April, 1954; the second, in January, 1957; the third, in September, 1961.

[3] See Marjorie C. Johnston, *Modern Foreign Languages in the High School,* U.S. Department of Health, Education, and Welfare, OE–27005 (Washington, D.C.: United States Government Printing Office, 1958).

administering those sections which pertained to modern foreign languages. Kenneth Mildenberger became Chief of the Language Development Section in 1959. His office and other sections within the Office of Education initiated several broad programs under the NDEA directed toward improving modern foreign language teaching.

Foundation grants aid research. In addition to federal funds, grants from three major foundations greatly accelerated the research in modern foreign languages. The Rockefeller Foundation's grant of $135,000 to the Modern Language Association over a period of approximately six years has already been cited. The Ford Foundation made a grant of $55,600 in 1959 to the MLA for a Center for Applied Linguistics, which had been established in Washington. In 1961 this same foundation gave the Center an additional grant of $1,300,000 to extend over a five-year period.

The Carnegie Corporation of New York, for several years a sponsor of the MLA's Foreign Language Program, granted $187,-000 to the MLA in 1961, over a three-year period, for four projects: (1) a repository of teaching materials in New York City where teachers could come and examine textbooks, tapes, records, and audio-visual equipment; (2) a foreign language specialist available to schools for consultation on language laboratories or other matters related to the teaching of foreign languages; (3) studies of the background and training of foreign language teachers in several states; (4) evaluation of the graduate-school preparation of prospective college language teachers.

Languages for the academically talented. Further emphasis on foreign language study for the academically able students was given by the joint report of the National Education Association and the Modern Language Association, *Modern Foreign Languages and the Academically Talented Student.*[4] This report recommended a program of foreign language study which would begin early in the grades and continue through high school. James B. Conant in his study of the American high schools had previously recommended four years of one foreign language in the programs of the academically talented.[5]

_____

[4] Edited by Wilmarth H. Starr, Mary P. Thompson, and Donald D. Walsh (Washington, D.C.: National Education Association of the United States, 1960).
[5] James Bryant Conant, *The American High School Today* (New York: McGraw-Hill Book Company, 1959), p. 57.

Numerous other publications helped inform the American public of the importance of foreign languages and the new techniques which were effective for their learning. The extent of the research on language teaching can be seen by consulting a bibliography compiled at the University of Washington, under contract with the United States Office of Education.[6] So much research on the improvement of foreign language teaching was in progress in 1960 that the Educational Press Association noted the fact as one of the ten major educational events for the year.

Results of research: the emerging of a profession. Under contract with the United States Office of Education and in consultation with the Educational Testing Services, the Modern Language Association constructed proficiency tests for the five commonly taught foreign languages. The MLA Proficiency Tests for Teachers and Advanced Students were administered for the first time in NDEA Summer Institutes in 1960 (see Chapter V). The construction of these tests between September, 1959, and June, 1960, was a remarkable achievement of approximately 100 dedicated language specialists, under the direction of Wilmarth H. Starr. Alternate test forms were subsequently constructed, and national norms were established from the scores made by teachers who took them in the 1960 and 1961 Language Institutes. With proficiency tests, language teachers now had means for evaluating a prospective teacher's eligibility for being admitted to the language teaching profession, and a sense of "profession" was beginning to emerge as wider use was made of these tests on a national scale.

Modern Spanish.[7] The first basic, audio-lingual language textbook for college use, *Modern Spanish,* appeared in 1960. Supported by funds from the MLA, a group of Spanish scholars designed a textbook according to scientific linguistic principles. *Modern Spanish* had widespread adoption and met with notable success wherever it was used in connection with a language laboratory. It set the pattern for many subsequent language textbooks.

Contrastive language analyses. The Center for Applied Lin-

---

6 Howard Lee Nostrand, *et al., Research on Language Teaching: An Annotated International Bibliography for 1945–61* (Seattle, Wash.: University of Washington Press, 1962).

7 Modern Language Association, *Modern Spanish* (New York: Harcourt, Brace & World, Inc., 1960).

guistics, a branch of the Modern Language Association in Washington, sponsored a series of ten volumes on contrastive studies. There are two volumes each for French, German, Italian, Russian, and Spanish. One volume presents the sound system and the other gives the structure of the foreign language under consideration; each volume contrasts English with the foreign language. This series, under the general editorship of Charles A. Ferguson and published by the University of Chicago Press, has the following authors: French, André Martinet and Stanley Lampach; German, Herbert Kufner and William G. Moulton; Italian, Frederick B. Agard and Robert di Pietro; Russian, William W. Gage; Spanish, Robert P. Stockwell, J. Donald Bowen, and John W. Martin.

Film series on language. In cooperation with the Teaching Film Custodians of New York City, the Modern Language Association produced a series of five 16 mm films on the principles and methods of teaching a foreign language. Each film is in black and white and requires 30 minutes for showing. The titles are as follows:

1. The Nature of Language and How It is Learned
2. The Sounds of Language
3. The Organization of Language
4. Words and Their Meanings
5. Modern Techniques in Language Teaching

These films are available for rental or purchase.

Surveys and studies. Reports of Surveys and Studies in the Teaching of Modern Foreign Languages,[8] discussed in Chapter V, was another landmark of research progress. Also, the MLA's revised *Selective List of Materials for Use by Teachers of Modern Foreign Languages in Elementary and Secondary Schools*[9] highlighted again that the final end of research in foreign languages was to improve the teaching of them.

A helpful reference list of source materials for junior and senior high school teachers was compiled in the United States Office of Education by specialists in foreign languages.[10] The list carries many entries on professional instructional materials of recent years: for example—audio-visual aids, course outlines and guides, cultural

---

[8] Modern Language Association, *op. cit.,* 1961.

[9] Modern Language Association, *op. cit.,* 1962.

[10] Esther M. Eaton, Mary E. Hayes, and Lynne L. Norton, *Source Materials for Secondary School Teachers of Foreign Languages,* OE–27001B, Circular No. 690 (Washington, D.C.: United States Government Printing Office, 1962).

aids from travel and information services, evaluation and testing, language laboratories, linguistics, teaching machines, textbooks, and vocational opportunities.

Another study of importance was the 1959 survey of Foreign Languages in Public Secondary Schools made by the United States Office of Education by means of a sampling technique. Questionnaires were sent to 3,255 secondary school principals, representing a probability sample of the approximately 23,800 schools which reported in the public secondary schools survey of 1958–59, and replies were received from 2,980 principals (92 per cent). Highlights from the report on the study follow:[11]

> The first national survey of foreign languages made through principals of public secondary schools reveals that in fall, 1959, 22 per cent of all public secondary school students in grades 7–12 were studying foreign language. The schools in which these students were enrolled represented 66 per cent of all public secondary schools.
>
> The highest enrollment occurred in Spanish, Latin, and French, in that order, followed by much lower counts for German and Italian. Other languages with less than one-half of one per cent of total language enrollment were Chinese, Czech, Greek (both classical and modern), Hebrew, Japanese, Norwegian, Polish, Portuguese, Russian, and Swedish.
>
> Of 34,000 foreign language teachers in the public secondary schools, 72 per cent were full-time employees. Only 57 per cent were teaching in the foreign language field alone.
>
> Data published by the Modern Language Association for language enrollment in the 7th and 8th grades in *elementary* schools in fall, 1959, have been combined with the data of this survey for the same grades in *secondary* schools, thus providing for the first time a full picture of language teaching at the 7th- and 8th-grade levels.

The number of foreign language students enrolled in the seventh and eighth grades, all sizes of secondary schools, was 226,349: seventh grade, 86,977; eighth grade, 139,372. The total of foreign language students in grades seven and eight constituted nine per cent of the total foreign language enrollment in the public secondary schools: seventh grade, 3.5 per cent; eighth grade, 5.6 per cent.[12]

---

[11] Esther M. Eaton, *Foreign Languages in Public Secondary Schools: Interim Report* (Washington, D.C.: United States Government Printing Office, 1963).
[12] *Ibid.*, Table 18.

Foreign language department within the National Education Association. In June, 1961, the NEA authorized the establishment of a Department of Foreign Languages. Many language teachers thought that such a department in the NEA would better disseminate information to elementary and secondary school teachers than had the more specialized journals of language organizations. The Department proposed to be a centralizing agency, speaking for the classical and modern language teachers, and acting as a clearinghouse for information and consultative services in the United States and abroad.

At the close of the decade. At the end of 1962, foreign language study in the United States was receiving unprecedented support from the general public, the Federal Government, and philanthropic foundations. Elementary and secondary schools were making possible longer sequences of language study, and institutions of higher learning were beginning to institute programs for the improvement of college teachers. Federal funds had provided mechanical aids for the classrooms (chiefly electronic language laboratories); institutes for the upgrading of teachers; study abroad for these teachers through the Cultural Exchange Act of 1961— a broadening of the Fulbright and Smith-Mundt acts; and millions of dollars for research designed to inform the teacher of the best techniques in teaching, to provide him with effective audio-lingual teaching materials, and to give the language profession proficiency tests by which to evaluate the teaching and learning processes. Foundation funds continued to help language organizations and individual researchers to advance the understanding of the nature of language—of how sound modulations form a system of communication for different ethnic groups—and to provide centers where consultative services and teaching materials were available to the teachers.

The best available technological advances had been grafted to the information on language and language-learning techniques. At the close of this decade of progress, leaders of the modern language groups were still stressing the audio-lingual approach to language learning, but they were also stressing that beyond the "approach" lie the ultimate humanistic goals: knowledge of a foreign literature and a foreign culture which give an understanding of a foreign people, toward the attainment of which the language is an indispensable tool.

Bibliography

Bagster-Collins, E. W., *et al.*, "Studies in Modern Language Teaching," *Reports Prepared for the Modern Foreign Language Study and the Canadian Committee on Modern Languages*, Vol. XVII. New York: The Macmillan Company, 1930.

Brooks, Nelson, *Language and Language Learning*. New York: Harcourt, Brace & World, Inc., 1960.

Childers, J. Wesley, "Foreign Language Offerings and Enrollments in Public Secondary Schools, Fall 1959," *Reports of Surveys and Studies in the Teaching of Modern Foreign Languages*. New York: Modern Language Association, 1961. Pp. 15–33.

Cole, Robert D., *Modern Foreign Languages and Their Teaching*. New York: Appleton-Century-Crofts, Inc., 1931.

Coleman, Algernon, *Experiments and Studies in Modern Language Teaching*. Chicago: University of Chicago Press, 1934.

———, *An Analytical Bibliography of Modern Language Teaching*. Chicago: The University of Chicago Press, 1938.

Eaton, Esther M., Mary E. Hayes, and Lynne L. Norton, *Source Materials for Secondary School Teachers of Foreign Languages*, OE–27001B, Circular No. 690. Washington, D.C.: United States Government Printing Office, 1962.

Harmon, John and Hannelore Tierney, *Modern Foreign Language Enrollments in Four-Year Colleges and Universities, Fall 1961*. New York: Modern Language Association, 1962.

Hutchinson, Joseph C., *Modern Foreign Languages in High School: The Language Laboratory*, U.S. Department of Health, Education, and Welfare, Bulletin 1961, No. 23. Washington, D.C.: United States Government Printing Office, 1961.

Johnston, Marjorie C., ed., *Modern Foreign Languages in the High School*, U.S. Department of Health, Education, and Welfare, OE–27005. Washington, D.C.: United States Government Printing Office, 1958.

Leavitt, Sturgis E., "The Teaching of Spanish in the United States," in *Reports of Surveys and Studies in the Teaching of Modern Foreign Languages*. New York: Modern Language Association, 1961. Pp. 309–26.

Matthew, Robert John, *Language and Area Studies in the Armed Services*. Washington, D.C.: American Council on Education, 1947.

Méras, Edmond A., *A Language Teacher's Guide*. New York: Harper & Row, Publishers, 1954.

Mildenberger, Kenneth W., *Status of Foreign Language Study in American Elementary Schools, Fall Term, 1953*. Washington, D.C.: United States Government Printing Office, 1954.

Modern Foreign Language Study, "Publication of the American and Canadian Committees on Modern Languages." Seventeen numbered volumes plus "A Summary of Reports on the Modern Foreign Languages." New York: The Macmillan Company; and Toronto: University of Toronto Press, 1927–31.

Modern Language Association of America, "Qualification for Secondary School Teachers of Modern Foreign Languages," *PMLA,* LXX, No. 4, Part II (September, 1955), 46–49.

————, *Reports of Surveys and Studies in the Teaching of Modern Foreign Languages by the Modern Language Association of America, 1959–1961.* New York: Modern Language Association, 1961.

Newmark, Maxim, *Twentieth Century Modern Language Teaching.* New York: The Philosophical Library, 1948.

Northeast Conference on the Teaching of Foreign Languages, ed., Seymour L. Flaxman, *Modern Language Teaching in School and College.* Princeton, N.J.: Princeton University Press, 1961.

Nostrand, Howard Lee, Sol Saporta, Judith Ann Milligan, Janet Hartwich Miller, John Alden Green, Doris Margaret Glasser, David William Foster, and Beverly J. Payne, *Research on Language Teaching: An Annotated International Bibliography for 1945–61.* Seattle, Wash.: University of Washington Press, 1962.

Ollmann, Mary J., ed., *MLA Selective List of Materials for Use by Teachers of Modern Foreign Languages in Elementary and Secondary Schools.* New York: Modern Language Association, 1962.

Palmer, Harold E., *The Oral Method of Teaching Languages.* New York: Harcourt, Brace & World, Inc., 1926.

Parker, William R., *The National Interest and Foreign Languages,* 3rd ed., United States National Commission for the United Nations Educational, Scientific, and Cultural Organization. Washington, D.C.: United States Government Printing Office, 1961.

Stack, Edward M., *The Language Laboratory and Modern Language Teaching.* New York: Oxford University Press, 1960.

Starr, Wilmarth H., Mary P. Thompson, and Donald D. Walsh, eds., *Modern Foreign Languages and the Academically Talented Student.* Washington, D.C.: National Education Association of the United States, 1960.

U.S. Department of Health, Education, and Welfare, *National Defense Language Development Research and Studies, Fiscal 1962,* OE–12014–62. Washington, D.C.: U.S. Government Printing Office, 1962.

Vamos, Mara, John Harmon, Hannelore Fischer-Lorenz, and Frank White, "Modern Foreign Language Enrollments in Four-Year Colleges and Universities, Fall 1960," in *Reports of Surveys and Studies in the Teaching of Modern Foreign Languages.* New York: Modern Language Association, 1961. Pp. 91–125.

Zeydel, Edwin H., "The Teaching of German in the United States from Colonial Times to the Present," in *Reports of Surveys and Studies in the Teaching of Modern Foreign Languages.* New York: Modern Language Association, 1961. Pp. 285–308.

V

Vamos, Mara, 10, 105
Vander Beke, George E., 36
Viëtor, Wilhelm, 32
Vocabulary, 33, 35, 36
Voice of America, 20
Voltaire, 12

W

Walsh, Donald D., 4, 10, 15, 19, 27, 108, 109
Walter, Max, 32
Wars and U. S. language enrollments:
France and Germany, 14, 16
Mexico and the United States, 17

Wars and U. S. language enrollments (*Cont.*)
Spain and the United States, 17
World War I, 2, 3, 8, 18, 32, 33
World War II, 3, 16, 18, 86, 107
Weidner, Edward W., 106
Wellemeyer, John Fletcher, 20
West, Michael, 56
Wheeler, C. A., 35
Wood, Ben D., 35, 64
Word lists, 33, 35, 36
Works Project Administration, 43
Writing, 53

Z

Zeydel, Edwin H., 7, 9